Friends

Activity Book 2

Carol Skinner

with **Liz Kilbey**

Language Diary

① **I can write my own examples.**

Present Simple	Examples
positive	He usually goes to a football match on Saturdays.
	1 I often ....
negative	Jenny doesn't write letters to the Londoners.
	2 ....
questions	Do you play football?
	3 ....

② **I know these words:**

park	country
ice rink	town
museum	capital
cinema	part
swimming pool	pen friend
zoo	match (n)

Vocabulary

1 **Match.**

1 park   d
2 ice rink
3 museum
4 cinema
5 swimming pool
6 zoo

2 Complete. Use the words in the box.

> country   town   capital   match
> pen friend   ~~part~~

1 Scotland is .part. of Great Britain.
2 London is the .... of England and Great Britain.
3 I often write to my .... in Spain.
4 Australia is a beautiful ....
5 Is there a football .... on TV tonight?
6 My best friend lives in a small .... in Spain.

Grammar

3 Write the sentences. Use the information in the chart.

	Often	Every week	X
1 play tennis	Mark	Vicki	Mark's parents
2 watch football matches	Rob	Mark	Vicki
3 eat pizza	Rob's family	Vicki and Kim	Kim's mum

1 *Mark often plays tennis.*
  Vicki plays tennis every week.
  Mark's parents don't play tennis.

2 ....
  ....
  ....
  ....

3 ....
  ....
  ....

4 Answer the questions. Use short answers.

1 Do you usually get up at six o'clock?
  No, I don't.

2 Do you often ride a bike?
  ....

3 Do you and your friends go to an indoor swimming pool?
  ....

4 Does your best friend often visit you?
  ....

5 Does your English teacher give you a lot of homework?
  ....

5 Complete. Use the Present Simple.

A Who (visit) [1].does.... Rob .visit..... in Italy?
B He (visit) [2]........... his grandparents.

A (go) [3]........... Jenny .... to the Londoners' school?
B No, she doesn't. She (go) [4].............. to a school in Australia.

A What (send) [5]........... Jenny .... to the Londoners?
B She (send) [6]........... emails but she (not / send) [7].................. letters.

A When (go) [8]........... Mark .... to a football match?
B He (go) [9]........... to a football match on Saturdays.

A Where (go) [10]........... the Londoners sometimes .... in London?
B They (go) [11]........... to the ice rink or the cinema.

A (like) [12]........... Kim .... swimming?
B Yes, she does, but she (not / like) [13]........................ swimming under water.

Use your English

6 Complete. Use the correct form of the words in CAPITALS.

1 My mum's parents are my .grandparents. .   PARENTS
2 Mark is a ....   LONDON
3 Vicki is a good ....   SWIM
4 Rob's grandparents are ....   ITALY
5 I don't like diving in the .... pool.   SWIM
6 We go to an .... ice rink in our town.   DOOR

2 Crazy Detectives

Language Diary

1 I can write my own examples.

Present Continuous	Examples
Positive	Today we are cleaning the house. **1** I'm .... now.
negative	Mrs Smith isn't polishing the furniture. **2** ....
questions	Is Mrs Smith wearing a coat? **3** ....

2 I know these words and expressions:

housework
polish
dust
sweep
vacuum
wash up
clean
do the washing

Vocabulary

1 Match.

1 do the washing   b
2 dust the ornaments   ☐
3 vacuum the carpet   ☐
4 polish the furniture   ☐
5 wash up   ☐
6 sweep the floor   ☐
7 clean the windows   ☐

Grammar

2 Write true sentences. What's happening now?

1 My mum / clean the house
My mum's cleaning the house. .... or
My mum isn't cleaning the house. ....

2 I / do / my English homework
....

3 I / wear / jeans
....

4 The birds / sing
....

5 I / write a letter
....

6 I / have / breakfast
....

7 It / rain
....

3 Look at all the pictures in Exercise 1. Write the questions and short answers.

1 Clueless / dust the ornaments
Is Clueless dusting the ornaments? ....
No, he isn't.

2 Mrs Smith / vacuum the carpets
....?
....

3 Clueless / wash up
....?
....

4 Mrs Smith / do the washing
....?
....

5 Holmes and Clueless / sweep the floor
....?
....

6 Holmes / polish the furniture
....?
....

7 Clueless / clean the windows
....?
....

4 Look at the picture and correct the sentences.

1 Holmes is talking to Mrs Smith.
Holmes isn't talking to Mrs Smith. ....
She's talking to Clueless. ....

2 Clueless is reading a book.
....
....

3 Clueless is drinking lemonade.
....
....

4 Holmes and Clueless are singing.
....
....

5 Mrs Smith is vacuuming the carpet.
....
....

Use your English

5 Circle the correct words.

Clueless   What are you ¹*doing* / *do* Mrs Smith?

Mrs Smith   I ²*am* / *is* sweeping the floor. What's Ms Holmes doing?

Clueless   She ³*are* / *is* looking at the furniture and shouting.

Mrs Smith   ⁴*When* / *Why* is she looking at the furniture?

Clueless   Because she's looking ⁵*on* / *for* fingerprints.

Mrs Smith   And why is she shouting?

Clueless   Because I'm ⁶*vacuuming* / *polishing* the furniture.

3

Language Diary

1 **I can complete the table and write my own examples.**

Stative verbs
like, *need* ....
....

Examples
Pandas like bamboo.
1 *I don't need ...* ....
2 ....
3 ....
4 ....

2 **I know these words:**

countryside	lake	dry
village	hills	bamboo
mountain	river	rice
desert	rocky	panda
field		

Vocabulary

1 **Look at the picture and complete.**

In the north there's a high ¹m*ountain*......... . A long
²r........................ goes into a big ³l........................ .
In the west there's a small ⁴v........................ and
there are some ⁵f........................ near it. In the east
there are some rocky ⁶h........................ and in the
south there's a ⁷d........................ .

2 Complete. Use the words in the box.

countryside pandas bamboo dry ~~rice~~

1 The Chinese grow a lot of .rice....... .

2 There is beautiful .... with green fields and tall trees, outside my town.

3 The Chinese cut down the .... in their country because they need new fields.

4 .... are pretty because their faces are white and their ears, eyes and noses are black.

5 It doesn't rain very often in this area and it's very ....

Grammar

3 Write the questions and answers. Use the Present Simple or the Present Continuous.

1 What (do) .are.......... you doing..... now?
I'm ....

2 (do) .... you .... this exercise with a friend?
....

3 (write) .... you .... with a pen or a pencil now?
....

4 What (think) .... you .... about your class?
....

5 What (like) .... you .... about your school?
....

6 When (feel) .... you .... happy?
....

7 What (wear) .... you .... at the moment?
....

8 (remember) .... you .... your first English lesson?
....

9 (understand) .... you .... all the questions in this exercise?
....

10 (need) .... you .... a dictionary?
....

4 Complete. Use the Present Simple or the Present Continuous.

It is Monday morning and Ta-Ming and his friend (walk)
¹.are walking.. to school. Ta-Ming (like) ²........... his school. He always (feel) ³...........
happy on Mondays because he (have) ⁴........... Art on that day. It's his favourite subject at school. Ta-Ming (talk) ⁵...............
to his friend about the future. He (want) ⁶........... to teach Art one day.

Use your English

5 Circle the correct answer – A, B or C.

Ta-Ming's mother works in the rice fields ¹............. . She likes her work. She ²............ all the workers. Ta-Ming's father ³............. works in the fields too but today he ⁴............ bamboo on the mountain near the village. Ta-Ming's father feels sad. He ⁵............ this work. He understands the farmers want fields to grow rice but the pandas ⁶............ food too.

1 A now   B today   C (every day)
2 A knows   B is knowing   C know
3 A now   B never   C often
4 A cuts down B is cutting down C cut down
5 A is hating B hate   C hates
6 A need   B needs   C are needing

4 Story Time

Language Diary

1 I can complete the table with sentences a–f.

Present Simple	Present Continuous
1 ~~I walk to school every day.~~	**4** ....
2	**5** ....
3	**6** ....

a I walk to school every day.

b What is she wearing today?

c My brother doesn't play football very often.

d Look! He's talking to the headmaster.

e The children always meet at break time.

f They're listening to their new CD.

2 I know these words:

pitch	headmaster	oxygen
league	pupil	carbon dioxide
team	insect	berries
captain	nut	squirrel

Vocabulary

1 Put the words in the correct groups.

> ~~pitch~~ ~~lessons~~ league captain cup
> headmaster team pupils teacher

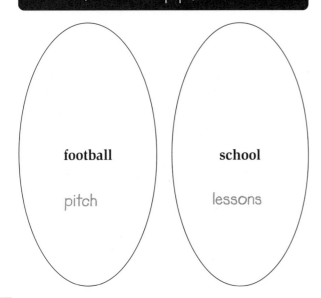

football

pitch

school

lessons

2 Complete. Use the words in the box.

> nuts carbon dioxide oxygen ~~insect~~
> berries squirrel

1 An ..insect...... has six legs.

2 A .... is an animal with a long tail.

3 Animals, plants and people need ....
to live.

4 Trees take .... from the air.

5 Animals in the woods often eat ....
and ....

Grammar

3 Complete. Use the Present Simple or the Present Continuous.

Julie Look, it's nine o'clock and the classroom is empty.

Kathy Well, the whole school's in the main hall now. They (listen) ¹are listening to the headmaster. He (talk) ²................. about our school football team. The football team's really good this year. The players (practise) ³................. every day.

Julie Yes, I know. My brother (practise) ⁴................. for four hours every afternoon. Then he (watch) ⁵................. football on TV. He's football crazy! Let's go to the hall!

Kathy Look, the headmaster (give) ⁶................. a cup to the team!

4 Put the words in the correct order to make questions. Then read the story and look at the picture in the Student's Book on page 10 and answer the questions.

1 start   at nine o'clock   lessons   do   at   Westpark school

Do lessons start at nine o'clock at Westpark school?
Yes, they do.

2 the pupils   listening   now   are   to their   headmaster

.... ?
....

3 talking   to the pupils   the headmaster   is

.... ?
....

4 sitting down now   the football team   are

.... ?
....

5 practise   every day   does   football   Sam

.... ?

6 watch   Julie's brother   football   does   often   on TV

.... ?

7 is   football   now   playing   Sam

.... ?
....

5 Write the questions and answers.

1 What / you / usually / have / for breakfast
What do you usually have for breakfast?
I usually drink ....

2 What time / your school / start
.... ?
....

3 you / often / eat / chocolate
.... ?
....

4 you / eat / chocolate / now
.... ?
....

5 How many / languages / you / speak
.... ?
....

6 What language / you / study / now
.... ?
....

Use your English

6 Circle the correct words.

Today Tim and Sam ¹*are playing* / *play* football in the park. They are great footballers. Sam ²*always* / *now* scores a lot of goals. Tim usually ³*stops* / *is stopping* all the shots at the goal. Now the game is over and the boys ⁴*sit* / *are sitting* under the trees. They ⁵*watch* / *are watching* a squirrel in the tree. It ⁶*eats* / *is eating* nuts.

Check Yourself

Units 1 – 4

Vocabulary

1 Match.

0 dust   `c`   **a** the carpets
1 vacuum   ☐   **b** a mess
2 do   ☐   **c** the ornaments
3 make   ☐   **d** the furniture
4 polish   ☐   **e** the floor
5 sweep   ☐   **f** the washing

Total ☐ 5

2 Circle the odd one out.

0 headmaster (parent) detective housekeeper
1 hills   fields   mountains   country
2 lake   city   town   village
3 polish   swim   clean   vacuum
4 nuts   squirrel   berries   leaves
5 ice rink   football   swimming pool   cinema

Total ☐ 5

Grammar

3 Make the sentences negative.

0 Girls usually play football.
    Girls don't usually play football.

1 We are listening to the headmaster now.
    ....

2 They speak English at work.
    ....

3 The Londoners live in Wales.
    ....

4 I'm doing my Maths homework now.
    ....

5 A panda eats rice.
    ....

6 She's sleeping at the moment.
    ....

Total ☐ 6

4 Circle the correct answers.

0 (Does John walk)/ Is John walking to school every day?
1 Do they clean / Are they cleaning the house today?
2 Look! My friend comes / is coming!
3 Listen! Who shouts / is shouting?
4 Does your friend play / Is your friend playing football on Saturdays?
5 Jane makes / is making a chocolate cake now.
6 I do / I'm doing the washing at the weekends.
7 Where do they go / are they going now?
8 Where do you go / are you going every summer?

Total ☐ 8

5 Complete. Use the correct form of the verbs in the box.

> hear   wear   ~~like~~   ring   clean   need
> live   snow   cut down

0 I (not) ...don't like... sad films.
1 .... you .... a dictionary?
2 Listen! The telephone ....
3 Why .... you .... jeans today?
4 It (not) .... every year in my country.
5 Look, the workmen .... trees.
6 He .... in the north of England.
7 Today I .... my room.
8 We often .... birds in the morning.

Total ☐ 16

Vocabulary ☐ 10
Grammar ☐ 30
Total ☐ 40

Skills Corner 1

Reading

1 Look at the picture and read the text. Guess the meaning of the words in the box from the context.

> invitations   theme   prepare
> sleep-over party

<u>Parties</u> by Sandy Smith, Class 6a

1 I like parties because I can talk with my friends, dance and eat good food. I also like preparing for parties. It's fun to make invitations, cook the food and plan the music and games.

2 Theme parties are my favourite. You choose a theme for your party and your friends wear clothes to match the theme. You can also decorate the party room and have food and music with the same theme. Fancy dress parties, funny hat parties and pyjama parties are also great fun!

3 My friends and I also like sleep-over parties. At sleep-over parties my girl friends eat and play games in my bedroom. Then they sleep at my house. Of course we go to sleep very late because we tell stories and talk about our friends for a long time.

4 Outdoor parties are also good – but you need good weather! My family and friends often have barbecues in a garden or on the beach. Food always tastes fantastic outdoors! Then we swim or play games. Sometimes my friends and I sleep in tents after these parties.

5 Tonight is my birthday party and the theme of the party is China. Today my mum is cooking Chinese food. I'm cleaning the house, decorating the party room and making my costume! I'm having fun!

2 Which paragraph tells you …

a about outdoor parties?   `4`

b why Sandy loves parties?   ☐

c about preparing for Sandy's birthday party?   ☐

d about theme parties?   ☐

e about sleep-over parties?   ☐

Writing

3 You are going to write a paragraph about your birthday parties. Tick ✓ the best topic sentence for your paragraph.

1 My friend loves parties.   ☐

2 I never go to sleep-over parties.   ☐

3 Every year I have a party for my birthday.   ☐

4 Write a paragraph about your birthday parties. Use the sentence from Exercise 3 to start your paragraph.

....
....
....
....
....
....
....
....
....
....
....
....
....
....
....
....

5 The LONDONERS

Language Diary

1 I can write my own examples.

Past Simple: *to be*	Examples
positive	His grandparents were poor. **1** I was ....
negative	My dad wasn't in London yesterday. **2** ....
questions	Were you at school yesterday? **3** ....

Past Simple: *there is / there are*	Examples
positive	There was a lot of traffic. **1** ....
negative	There weren't any buses in 1700. **2** ....
questions	Was there a swimming pool at your school? **3** ....

2 I know these words:

street
roundabout
office block
traffic
traffic lights
zebra crossing
open top bus
double-decker bus
horse-drawn carriage

Vocabulary

1 Label the picture.

1	..........street..........	2	....	3	....	4	....
5	....	6	....	7	....	8	....

Grammar

2 Complete. Use *was, wasn't, were* or *weren't*.

Rob Where ¹..were.... you born, Kim?

Kim I ²............ born in England. But my dad's from Wales.

Rob Oh, my dad's from Italy.

Kim Really? And you and your sisters?

Rob I ³............ born there but my sisters ⁴............ born in Great Britain.

Kim Have you got grandparents in Italy?

Rob Yes, I have. They ⁵............ here last week for a holiday. But they ⁶............ happy.

Kim Why?

Rob Because the weather ⁷............ bad and they don't like the pizzas in England!

3 Complete. Use *there was / were, there wasn't / weren't*.

Last week Mark was at an exhibition of photos of London with his dad. ¹..There were.. some old black and white photos of London in the nineteenth century. ²..................... also a lot of great photos of London now. ³..................... a good photo of Piccadilly Circus at night. ⁴..................... one person in the photo and (not) ⁵..................... a lot of traffic.

4 Write the questions.

Rob ¹..Were you born.. in Rome, Dad?

Dad No, I was born in a village near Rome.

Rob ²................................... ?

Dad No, it wasn't a big village but it was very pretty.

Rob ³................................ in the village?

Dad Oh, there were about a thousand people. They were very friendly.

Rob ⁴.................................. at that time?

Dad No, there weren't any horse-drawn carriages! I'm not that old!

Rob ⁵................................ in those days?

Dad No, there weren't many cars in our village. Cars were very expensive.

Rob ⁶....................................... ?

Dad No, we weren't rich. There wasn't a lot of work and many people were poor.

Use your English

5 Circle the correct answer – A, B or C.

Kim Mum, ¹............ you a good pupil at school?

Mum Of course I was! Well, I wasn't very, very good!

Kim ²............ was your school?

Mum It ³............ in a small village near Edinburgh.

Kim How many pupils ⁴............ at your school?

Mum Oh, only about fifty. It wasn't a big school.

Kim ⁵............ your best friend from your class?

Mum Yes, she ⁶............ . We meet sometimes and look at the photos.

1	**A** was	**B** (were)	**C** where
2	**A** What	**B** When	**C** Where
3	**A** were	**B** is	**C** was
4	**A** were there	**B** there were	**C** weren't there
5	**A** Was	**B** Were	**C** Was there
6	**A** is	**B** was	**C** wasn't

6 Crazy Detectives

Language Diary

(1) I can complete the table.

Past Simple positive			
regular verbs		*irregular verbs*	
1 want	wanted	**1** know	knew
2 help	....	**2** have	....
3 listen	....	**3** put	....
4 work	....	**4** see	....
5 play	....	**5** say	....

(2) I know these words:

urgent	knock	thief
delicious	continue	pocket
wrong	decide	vase
surprised	telephone (v)	
	shout	

Vocabulary

1 Put the letters in the correct order.

Yesterday Mrs Smith went to a shop to buy a present for her grandson. It was **rugnet** 1 ...urgent... because his birthday party was in the evening. Mrs Smith wanted to buy a **iucilosed** 2................ chocolate cake. In the shop she looked into her **epctok** 3................ but her money wasn't there. She was very **pdsrisure** 4................ . She thought there was a **ifthe** 5................ in the shop but she was **rogwn** 6................ . Her money was in a **aevs** 7................ at home. Mrs Smith often hides her money there!

2 Complete. Use the words in the box.

> knock ~~continue~~ decide telephone shout

1 Holmes and Clueless often start a game of chess in the evening and ...continue... it the next day.

2 Please don't .... – I can hear you very well.

3 Look, the doorbell isn't working. We must .... at her door.

4 I never .... her at work.

5 I can't .... what to do tonight.

Grammar

3 Complete. Use the Past Simple.

Yesterday Mrs Smith (go) ¹.went....... to her grandson's birthday party. She (have) ²............... a chocolate cake for him. She (put) ³............... the cake on the kitchen table. Then she (hurry) ⁴............... into the hall and (telephone) ⁵............... her friend. At that moment her grandson's dog (see) ⁶............... the cake and (eat) ⁷............... it. Mrs Smith (come) ⁸............... back into the kitchen and (shout) ⁹............... at the dog. She was very angry but the dog was very happy!

4 Complete. Use the Past Simple of the verbs in the box.

> get on   take   ~~open~~   ask   decide   drink

1 Mrs Smith .opened... the window because it was very hot in the kitchen.
2 Last Sunday Clueless .... the wrong bus.
3 Mrs Smith .... some cola after dinner.
4 Last week a thief .... money from Mrs Smith's pocket.
5 Holmes .... the thief a lot of questions and then she .... to telephone the police.

5 Put the sentences in the correct order.

a Finally Mrs Smith went back home. ☐

b Last Saturday Mrs Smith decided to visit her sister. [1]

c After that she walked from the station to her sister's house. ☐

d First she walked to the station and there she got on a train to her sister's town. ☐

e Next she telephoned her sister but she wasn't at home. Her sister was on holiday. ☐

f Then she knocked at the door of her sister's house but there was no answer. ☐

Use your English

6 Complete. Use one word in each gap.

Yesterday Mrs Smith ¹.went.. to her sister's house so Clueless and Holmes ate sandwiches all day. They ²............... very hungry! In the evening the detectives ³............... chess and had some tea. Then they had an urgent phone call from Mrs Smith. ⁴............... were surprised because she wanted to see them at her sister's place. They hurried to her sister's house and they knocked ⁵............... the door. Mrs Smith opened the door and there ⁶............... a delicious meal on the table for them! What a surprise!

7 Friends' Club

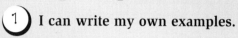

Language Diary

1 I can write my own examples.

Past Simple negative	Examples
regular	They didn't cook dinner yesterday. **1** _I didn't_ ....
irregular	They didn't swim in the river. **2** ....
questions	
regular	Did you do the washing up last night? **3** ....
irregular	Did they sleep in a tent? **4** ....

2 I know these words:

outdoor activities	equipment	canoe
camping	torch	paddle
walking	matches	life jacket
canoeing	sleeping bag	compass
	tent	walking boots
	map	rucksack
	helmet	

Vocabulary

1 Label the pictures.

①
.....helmet.....

②
....

③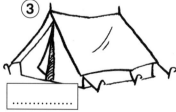
....

④
....

⑤
....

⑥
....

⑦
....

⑧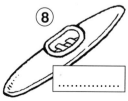
....

⑨
....

⑩
....

2 Circle the correct words.

1 Last night I used a *torch* / *paddle* to read in bed.

2 We wanted to find the nearest wood on our *map* / *compass*.

3 My favourite *equipment* / *outdoor activity* is swimming.

4 I don't like *camping* / *canoeing* because I hate sleeping in a tent.

5 My friends went *walking* / *canoeing* yesterday and lost their paddles.

Grammar

3 Write the questions and answers.

1 Annie's dad / cook / the meals
Did Annie's dad cook the meals?

2 Annie / swim / every morning
.... ?

3 Where / Annie's dad put up the tent
.... ?

4 Annie and her brother / wash up / after meals
.... ?

5 What / Annie / use to read at night
.... ?

6 Annie / enjoy / her camping holiday
.... ?

4 Make the sentences negative.

1 He read in bed last night.
He didn't read in bed last night.

2 His class went camping last year.
....

3 They put up the tent near a river.
....

4 My brother washed up after dinner.
....

5 I swam in the sea last summer.
....

6 The mosquitoes bit the children last night.
....

7 They slept in tents.
....

8 My parents enjoyed their last holiday.
....

Use your English

5 Circle the correct words.

Ally What ¹*do* / *did* you do last holiday?

Alex I went walking with a friend.

Ally What did you take with you?

Alex Well, we ²*take* / *took* rucksacks and we had walking ³*shoes* / *boots*. We had a compass and a map with us too so we always knew the way.

Ally Did you ⁴*have* / *had* a good time?

Alex Yes, it was a great holiday. But one night we decided to stay in the hills for the night. We put ⁵*on* / *up* a tent but then it started to rain! We didn't ⁶*enjoy* / *enjoyed* that night!

8 Story Time

Language Diary

1 I can complete the table with sentences a–g.

Present Simple

1 *They don't want to cut down the trees.*

2 ....

Present Continuous

3 ....

4 ....

Past Simple

5 ....

6 ....

7 ....

a We saw the workmen this morning.

b They aren't working now.

c They don't want to cut down the trees.

d The children didn't go to the wood.

e There were roads all around the buildings.

f What are you doing here?

g At lunch break we always meet our friends.

2 I know these words:

measure *(v)*	mark *(v)*	ground	receptionist
dry *(v)*	find out	lift *(n)*	drawing
cut down	reply *(v)*	cross *(n)*	

Vocabulary

1 Complete. Use the words in the box.

> ~~measure~~ cut down mark reply
> dry

1 Let's ..measure... the ground in the garden. I want to have a swimming pool there.

2 They want to .... the trees with red crosses.

3 We mustn't .... this tree. It's very old.

4 You can .... your wet football shirt in front of the fire.

5 My pen friend didn't .... to my letter.

2 Complete. Use the words in the box.

> ground drawing lift receptionist ~~crosses~~
> find out

At the lunch break Kathy, Julie, Tim and Sam went to Upton Wood. The workmen from the Brown's Building Company marked the trees with red [1].crosses. and measured the [2].............. .

After school the children went to the Brown's Building Company. They wanted to [3].............. about the plans for Upton Wood. First they talked to the [4].............. and then they took the [5].............. to the first floor. They went into Mr Brown's office and saw a large [6].............. on the wall.

Grammar

3 Complete. Use the correct form of the verbs in brackets.

Every day Sam and his friend Tim (play) ¹.play. football after school but today they (be) ²............ in Sam's house. They (talk) ³............ with Sam's sister, Julie, and her friend Kathy about Upton Wood. Yesterday the children (go) ⁴............ into Upton Wood and (see) ⁵............ the workmen there. Then they (visit) ⁶............ the Brown's Building Company and (look) ⁷............ at the plans for Upton Wood.

'It's terrible!' says Julie. 'Children (play) ⁸............ in Upton Wood and we all (like) ⁹............ walking there. It's a beautiful wood.'

'Yes,' says Sam. 'Now we (know) ¹⁰............ the truth. The workmen are in Upton Wood now because they (make) ¹¹............ the new football pitch there!'

4 Complete. Use the correct form of the verbs.

cut down

1 The workmen from the Brown's Building Company .cut down. a lot of trees yesterday.

2 They .... the trees now.

3 Building companies often .... trees.

ring

4 The school bell .... at nine o'clock last Monday.

5 Listen! The school bell .... for the end of lunch break.

6 .... the school bell always .... for afternoon lessons?

hide

7 Sam and his friends .... behind the trees now to watch the workmen.

8 Mr Brown usually .... the plans for Upton Wood in his desk but today they're on the wall.

9 The children .... the posters behind the trees and waited.

measure

10 The workmen .... the wood last week.

11 Look, they .... the old football pitch!

12 The workmen from the building company always .... the ground before they start working.

Use your English

5 Circle the correct answer – A, B or C.

my Favourite Places
by Julie, Class 7b

One of my favourite places is Upton Wood in my town. I often go there at the ¹........ with my family. Sometimes I ²........ my friends from school there too. Sometimes my best friend and I ³........ our homework there.

My other favourite place is my auntie's house. She ⁴........ in a small village in the countryside. I always ⁵........ fun in her garden with her three cats, two dogs and a pony! I ⁶........ there last year for three weeks. It was great!

	A		B		C	
1	A	week	B	weekend	C	day
2	A	met	B	are meeting	C	meet
3	A	doing	B	do	C	did
4	A	lives	B	is living	C	live
5	A	has	B	am having	C	have
6	A	stayed	B	stay	C	am staying

9 The LONDONERS

Language Diary

1 I can complete the table with sentences a–d.

Comparative of short adjectives	Superlative of short adjectives
1 I'm taller than you.	**3** ....
2	**4** ....

a I'm taller than you.

b He's the shortest boy in the class.

c This is the easiest way home.

d My hair is darker than yours.

2 I know these words:

shy	small	big	long
friendly	short	thin	
hard	tall	easy	
pretty	fat	ugly	

Vocabulary

1 Write the opposites. Then find them in the wordsquare. Look →↓.

1 long   short.....   **4** thin   ....

2 easy   ....   **5** ugly   ....

3 big   ....

r	a	s	m	a	l	l	y
f	a	t	r	y	p	s	o
s	t	s	h	o	r	t	n
h	s	m	a	r	e	f	a
a	r	d	r	g	t	g	g
i	p	r	d	t	t	y	s
a	l	s	h	o	y	t	y

2 Circle the correct words.

1 That girl is very *long* / *tall.*

2 People in this village never say 'hello'. They aren't very *friendly* / *hungry.*

3 He never goes near horses because he's *scared* / *proud* of them.

4 The dog is very *thin* / *fat* because it eats a lot of sweets.

5 I can't do this exercise. It's very *big* / *hard.*

6 He doesn't like going to parties because he's very *shy* / *friendly.*

Grammar

3 **Complete. Use the comparative or superlative of adjectives.**

The Londoners often go to Hyde Park because it's (near) ¹the nearest. park to their houses. The boys think it's (nice) ²........... park in London because it's got a beautiful lake. The lake is (big) ³........... than the lakes in many other parks. Yesterday the Londoners went to another park to have a picnic. The new park was (small) ⁴........... than Hyde Park and there wasn't a lake there. The girls thought it was (pretty) ⁵........... than Hyde Park but the boys didn't like it.

4 **Write the sentences. Use the comparative or superlative of adjectives.**

1 Wales / small / England
Wales is smaller than England.

2 The New Forest / big / forest in the south of England
The New Forest is the biggest forest in the south of England.

3 Vicki / short / Kim
....

4 Ponies / usually / fat / horses
....

5 Deer / shy / animals / in the New Forest
....

6 Maths / easy / subject / for Rob?
.... ?

7 Mark / tall / Rob
....

8 England / large / country / in Great Britain
....

5 **Complete and answer the questions.**

1 Which school subject is .easier. for you – Maths or English? (easy)
.Maths / English is easier for me than...... .English / Maths.

2 Who's .... person in your class? (friendly)
....

3 Is your best friend .... you? (tall)
....

4 Which is .... lesson at school for you? (hard)
....

5 Who has got .... hair in your class? (long)
....

6 Are you .... your best friend? (old)
....

7 Which is .... – a picnic in a forest or a picnic at the seaside? (nice)
....

Use your English

6 **Circle the correct words.**

Dear Auntie Sally,

I'm sending you a photo of my friend, Kim and me. Kim is a ¹new / newer girl in my class. She's ²a / the tallest girl in the class. Her father is from Wales. She says Wales is prettier ³than / from England.

Dad took this photo in the New Forest last week. The New Forest ponies are ⁴small / smaller than horses and very ⁵friendly / friendlier. There are a lot of deer in the New Forest but we didn't see them. It isn't easy to find them – they are very ⁶shy / shyer .

See you next week!

Lots of love,

Vicki

10 Crazy Detectives

Language Diary

1) I can complete the table with sentences a–d.

Comparative of long adjectives	Superlative of long adjectives
1 My clothes are more fashionable than yours.	3 ....
2	4 ....

a The queen has the most valuable jewels in England.

b My clothes are more fashionable than yours.

c Is your furniture more comfortable than mine?

d Holmes is the most famous detective in London.

2) I know these words:

burglary	fingerprints	valuable
burglar	steal	colourful
investigation	break into	expensive
clue	comfortable	important
detective	fashionable	

Vocabulary

1 Circle the correct words.

1 A (burglar) / burglary broke into my house last night.

2 The thieves *caught / stole* a lot of jewellery yesterday.

3 There were lots of *fingerprints / clues* on the furniture because the thief didn't wear gloves.

4 The detective found an important *burglary / clue* in the car.

5 The police started the *investigation / clue* last week.

6 Last summer there was a terrible *burglar / burglary* in my house.

7 I lost my car keys and decided to *steal / break* into my car.

2 Find four more adjectives in the word snake.

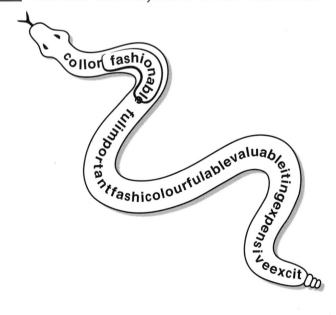

Grammar

3 Complete. Use the comparative or superlative of adjectives.

1 Who is ....the most famous. detective in England? (famous)

2 Holmes wears .... clothes than Mrs Smith. (fashionable)

3 It was .... investigation of the year. (important)

4 Is Holmes a .... detective than Clueless? (good)

5 Clueless bought .... hat in the shop. (expensive)

6 Is Clueless a .... singer than Holmes? (bad)

4 Write the sentences. Use the comparative of adjectives.

1 Brad Pitt / Britney Spears / famous
Brad Pitt is more famous than Britney Spears. or
Brad Pitt isn't more famous than Britney Spears.

2 Maths / English / difficult
....

3 wasps / flies / dangerous
....

4 the Queen's jewels / Holmes's jewels / valuable
....

5 detective stories / science fiction stories / interesting
....

6 camping / canoeing / exciting
....

7 a chair / a sofa / comfortable
....

5 Complete and answer the questions.

1 Who's ..the most famous.. pop star in your country? (famous)
....

2 Who's got .... clothes in your class? (colourful)
....

3 Which is .... school subject for you? (difficult)
....

4 Who's got .... hairstyle in your family? (fashionable)
....

5 Who's .... singer in your family? (bad)
....

6 Who's .... dancer in your family? (good)
....

7 What's .... TV programme for children in your country? (interesting)
....

Use your English

6 Complete. Use the correct form of the words in CAPITALS.

1 Holmes lives in .central. London. — CENTRE

2 My dress is more .... than hers. — COLOUR

3 Yesterday there was a .... at my friend's house. — BURGLAR

4 I've got some beautiful .... on my wall. — PAINT

5 There's a lot of very valuable .... in that house. — JEWEL

6 Her jacket is very .... — FASHION

11 Friends' Club

Language Diary

1 I can complete the table with the words below.

> **1** We use *the* for unique things and objects.
> the Moon, ...
>
> **2** We use *the* before the names of mountains, rivers, seas and oceans.
> ....
>
> **3** We use *the* before the superlative of adjectives.
> ....
>
> the South Pole, the North Pole, the most fashionable clothes,
> the Baltic Sea, the Andes, the wettest place, the Pacific Ocean

2 I can complete the sentences.

> **a / an / the / ø**
>
> There's .a......... high mountain near my town. I sometimes climb .... mountain with my friends.
>
> There are .... lakes near my town. We often swim in .... lakes in summer.

3 I know these words:

> ocean
> Moon
> sky
> Sun
> continent
> Equator
> North Pole
> South Pole
> mountain range

Vocabulary

1 Do the crossword.

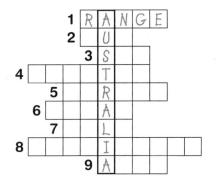

1 Where's the longest mountain .... in the world?
2 The .... gives light and heat to the Earth.
3 It's blue and you can see this above the Earth.
4 The .... is the hottest place on our planet.
5 A lot of elephants live in India and ....
6 An .... is bigger than a sea.
7 The North .... is one of the coldest places on our planet.
8 There are seven .... on our planet.
9 China, Japan and Russia are countries in ....

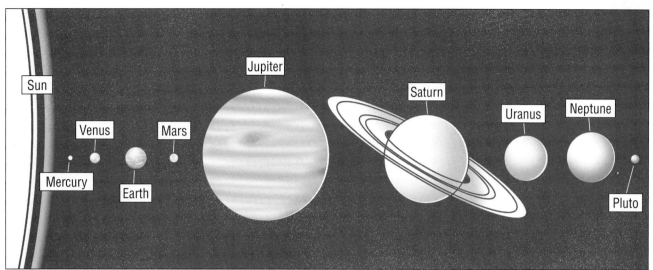

Labels in the image: Sun, Mercury, Venus, Earth, Mars, Jupiter, Saturn, Uranus, Neptune, Pluto

Grammar

2 Correct the sentences where necessary.

1 Asia is a largest continent.
   Asia is the largest continent.

2 Can you see the Moon tonight?
   ....

3 Andes are longest mountain range in the world.
   ....

4 Three quarters of Earth is water.
   ....

5 My friend lives in Africa.
   ....

6 How far is Sun from Earth?
   ....

7 Equator is hottest place on our planet.
   ....

3 Complete. Use *a*, *an* or *the* where necessary.

1 I live in ..a.. city not far from London.
   ..The.. city is called Oxford.

2 My dad's got .... photo of .... North Pole. .... photo is very old.

3 There is .... ocean between .... Europe and .... America. .... ocean is called .... Pacific Ocean.

4 There is .... ancient vase in my uncle's house. .... vase comes from Egypt.

5 I've just read .... interesting book. .... book is about some teenagers from London.

6 She's got .... cat. .... cat isn't very friendly.

Use your English

4 Circle the correct answer – A, B or C.

Dear Alex and Alley, The magazine about ¹............ Earth was very interesting. I knew all the answers. I also liked Pedro's letter about his village. I think Machu Picchu is ²............ .

I live in ³............ small village too. The village is in ⁴............ coldest part of Finland. It is near ⁵............ North Pole. I like my village but in the winter it's dark and cold because there is no ⁶............ and heat from the Sun.

Best wishes,

Paavo

1	**A** an	**B** the	**C** ø
2	**A** amazing	**B** ancient	**C** wet
3	**A** the	**B** ø	**C** a
4	**A** the	**B** a	**C** ø
5	**A** a	**B** ø	**C** the
6	**A** water	**B** light	**C** rain

(In item 1, answer B "the" is circled.)

12 Story Time

Language Diary

1 I can write my own examples.

going to	Examples
positive	He's going to telephone the police. **1** We're going to ....
negative	We aren't going to leave next week. **2** ....
questions	Are the workmen going to build a shopping centre here? **3** ....

2 I know these words:

reporter   cheer
photographer   march
workman   save
               move
               shout

Vocabulary

1 Complete. Use the words in the box.

> cheer ~~march~~ save move shout

1 I play the trumpet in a band. Sometimes we ..march.. through the town.

2 Please don't .... Your baby sister is sleeping.

3 It wasn't a very good football match and the fans didn't ....

4 Please .... your head, I can't see the TV.

5 I .... some money every week because I want to buy a bike.

2 Match. There is one extra definition.

1 headmaster   [c]
2 reporter   [ ]
3 workman   [ ]
4 photographer   [ ]
5 pupil   [ ]

a This person works with his hands.

b This person studies in a school.

c This man is a top person at school.

d This person writes books.

e This person writes stories for newspapers.

f This person takes photos.

Grammar

3 What's going to happen next week?
Look at Tim's diary and write the sentences.

Monday	talk to the reporter with Sam, Kathy and Julie
Tuesday	phone the photographer in the evening
Wednesday	play football with Sam
Thursday	meet Julie, Kathy and Sam at 11.00
Friday	go to a meeting with the people of the town and the headmaster
Saturday	play tennis with Julie
Sunday	study for a Biology test

1 The children *are going to talk to the reporter on Monday.*

2 Tim...
.... on Tuesday.

3 Sam and Tim..
.... on Wednesday.

4 Sam, Kathy, Julie and Tim ....
.... on Thursday.

5 On Friday Tim ....
....

6 Julie and Tim ....
.... on Saturday.

7 Tim..
.... on Sunday.

4 Write the questions and answers.
Use *going to*.

1 you / play / football / tonight
Are you going to play football tonight?
No, I'm not. / Yes, I am.

2 you / watch / television / tonight
.... ?
....

3 your best friend / come / to your house / today
.... ?
....

4 What time / you / get up / tomorrow morning
.... ?
....

5 your parents / visit / their friends / tonight
.... ?
....

6 What / you and your friends / do / at the weekend
.... ?
....

7 What / you / be / in the future
.... ?
....

Use your English

5 Complete.

Julie What great news! They aren't going to cut ¹..down.. the trees in Upton Wood!

Tim Yes, and we're going to use Westpark Stadium.

Julie ².......... you going to practise there?

Tim No, we ³........... . But we're going ⁴.......... play all the matches for the All-England schools league there. And ⁵.........'s more good news! We're going to have a big party at school next Saturday. The headmaster's ⁶......... to invite the players from Westpark Football Club and the people from the newspaper.

29

Check Yourself
Units 9 – 12

1 **Circle the odd one out.**

0 fashionable   comfortable   (terrible)   colourful

1 burglary   investigation   fingerprints   reporter

2 cheer   shout   march   talk

3 river   sea   mountain   ocean

4 short   shy   tall   fat

5 Sun   Moon   Equator   Earth

Total ☐ 5

2 **Write the opposites.**

0 easy - h a r d   **3** fat - t _ _ _

1 tall - s _ _ _ _   **4** ugly - p _ _ _ _ _

2 big - s _ _ _ _   **5** long - s _ _ _ _

Total ☐ 5

Grammar

3 **Write the comparative and the superlative of these adjectives.**

0 nice   ..nicer..   ..the nicest..

1 pretty   ....

2 colourful   ....

3 bad   ....

4 hot   ....

Total ☐ 8

4 **Correct the sentences.**

0 Andes are a very long mountain range.
  The Andes are a very long mountain range.

1 The Australia is a big continent.

  ....

2 You can see Moon tonight.

  ....

3 Who is best footballer in your class?

  ....

4 The Earth goes around Sun.

  ....

5 The Amazon is in the South America.

  ....

Total ☐ 5

5 **Complete. Use *a, an* or *the* where necessary.**

0 Here is ..a.. photo of my town. .The. photo is very old.

1 There is .... lake in my village. .... lake is very deep.

2 I love .... mountains!

3 'I'm going to see .... Atlantic Ocean this summer.'

4 Tonight we're going to see .... film about .... humpback whales.

5 .... sky is beautiful today!

6 Has she got .... son?

7 Are there .... deer in this forest?

Total ☐ 9

6 **Complete. Use the correct form of *going to*.**

A 0.Are. you going.to.. meet your friend tonight?

B No, I 0.'m not.... .

A 1.................. Mike .... have a party on Saturday?

B Yes, he 2.................. .

A What 3.................. you .... do in the summer?

B I 4.................. learn to swim.

A Where 5.................. they .... be at four o'clock?

B I'm (not) 6.................. tell you.

A 7.................. she .... see the film tonight?

B No, she 8.................. .

Total ☐ 8

Vocabulary	10
Grammar	30
Total	40

30

Skills Corner 3

Reading

1 Read Sandy's notes and divide her letter into five paragraphs.

paragraph 1	ask about uncle's holiday / my holiday - how long
paragraph 2	the village (small, near the sea, lake, nice shops)
paragraph 3	the food (ate octopus, olives - bought olive oil)
paragraph 4	what we did (boat trips, walking, open-air cinema)
paragraph 5	see Uncle Tod next weekend / bring photos

Dear Uncle Tod,

[I hope you are well and you had a nice holiday in Spain. We had a wonderful holiday in Greece. We were there for two weeks.] **1** We stayed in Ayios Nikolaos, a village in Crete. I think it's the prettiest village in Crete because it's near the sea and there's also a lake in the centre of it. There were lots of shops for the tourists there but many things were more expensive than in England. I really enjoyed the Greek food. I ate octopus and olives for the first time. We bought some delicious olive oil. The island is famous for it and I'm going to learn to cook with it. There were lots of things to do in Ayios Nikolaos. We swam in the sea and we went on boat trips. We also went for bicycle rides in the evenings but the best thing was the open-air cinema! I'm looking forward to seeing you next weekend. I'm going to bring you all my photos of my holiday and tell you more about it.

Best wishes,

Sandy

Writing

2 You are going to write a letter about your last holiday to your best friend. Plan the letter. Write notes for each paragraph. Look at Exercise 1 for ideas.

paragraph 1 ....
....
paragraph 2 ....
....
paragraph 3 ....
....
paragraph 4 ....
....

3 Use your notes in Exercise 2 and write the letter.

Dear .... ,
    How are you? I had a wonderful holiday
....
....
....
....
....
....
....
....
....
....
....
....
....
....
....
....
....
Best wishes, ...
....

13 The LONDONERS

Language Diary

(1) **I can write my own examples.**

have to	Examples
positive	They have to get up at six o'clock every day.
	1 _Students at my school have to_ ... .
negative	The Londoners don't have to go to school today.
	2 ....
questions	Does Rob have to meet Vicki today?
	3 ....

(2) **I know these words and expressions:**

It's brilliant!   arrange

You're hopeless!   queue (v, n)

You're so bossy!   camera

Lucky you!   cloakroom

It's amazing!   model

You're crazy!   visit (n)

Vocabulary

1 Match.

1 Mark's dad bought him a computer.   ☐ f

2 I can't find my money! I think I left it at home!   ☐

3 I can go with you to the cinema tonight!   ☐

4 We can't be late. Hurry up!   ☐

5 Look at that Alpha Romeo car!   ☐

6 I want to be thinner. I'm not going to have any dinner today.   ☐

a You're crazy!

b Yes, it's amazing!

c Oh, you're hopeless!

d You're so bossy!

e Brilliant!

f Lucky him!

2 Complete. Use the words in the box.

> visit   ~~camera~~   queue   model
> arrange   cloakroom

1 This ..camera.. takes wonderful photographs.

2 Rob and his dad made a .... of the new Alpha Romeo car.

3 The Londoners enjoyed their .... to Madame Tussaud's Museum last week.

4 You can put your coats and bags in the ....

5 My friends want to .... a trip to France.

6 The Londoners didn't .... to go into Madame Tussaud's Museum because they had tickets.

Grammar

3 Complete. Use the correct form of *have to* and a verb in the box.

~~take~~ meet work pay queue get up

1 We .have..to..take.. a bus to school.

2 Madame Tussaud's Museum is very popular so you always .... for tickets.

3 Rob .... his friends very early tomorrow.

4 We (not) .... for the cloakroom. It's free.

5 Her mum .... on Saturdays.

6 I (not) .... early at weekends.

4 Write the questions and answers about the Londoners. Use *have to*.

	Kim	Mark	Rob	Vicki
take a bus to school	✓	✓	✗	✗
clean his / her bedroom	✓	✓	✗	✓
take the dog for a walk	✗	✗	✓	✗
help in the garden	✓	✓	✓	✗

1 Who / take a bus to school
   Who has to take a bus to school?
   Kim and Mark have to take a bus
   to school.

2 Who / not clean his (her) bedroom / every week
   ....
   ....?

3 Who / take the dog for a walk
   ....?
   ....

4 Who / help in the garden
   ....?
   ....

5 Who / not help in the garden
   ....?
   ....

5 Answer the questions.

1 Do you have to take a bus to school?
   .Yes,.I.do../.No,.I.don't................

2 Do you have to go to bed early at weekends?
   ....

3 Does your best friend have to help with the housework?
   ....

4 Do your parents sometimes have to go to your school?
   ....

5 Do you have to clean your bedroom every day?
   ....

6 Do you have to study every day?
   ....

Use your English

6 Circle the correct answer – A, B or C.

Mark Rob, do you want to go to the Science Museum with me on Sunday? It's my birthday!

Rob Oh, yes, I ¹........ ! Good idea. Do we ²........ get there early to buy the tickets?

Mark No, it's free on Sundays so we ³........ buy tickets.

Rob Brilliant! Do we ⁴........ to take a bus there?

Mark No, we can walk or take our bikes.

Rob Good, because I ⁵........ got any money.

Mark ⁶........ , Rob. What happened to all your money?

Rob I bought a birthday present for you!

1 A want	B (do)	C am
2 A have	B have to	C has to
3 A haven't to	B not have to	C don't have to
4 A have	B had	C has
5 A haven't	B don't	C not
6 A Lucky you	B You're hopeless	C You're bossy

33

14 Crazy Detectives

 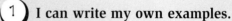

Language Diary

1 I can write my own examples.

will (prediction)	Examples
positive	Clueless will catch a fish this afternoon. **1** I will ....
negative	She won't marry you. **2** ....
questions	Will they visit another country? **3** ....

2 I know these words and expressions:

believe	fisherman
marry	husband
catch a cold	bunch
catch a fish	fortune teller
catch a thief	

Vocabulary

1 Do the crossword.

Across:

2 He caught a big .... in the river near his house.

7 It's raining and I haven't got a coat. I think I'm going to catch a ....

8 My brother loves the sea and he wants to be a ....

9 My dad is a very good detective. He caught a dangerous .... yesterday.

Down:

1 My father is my mother's ....

3 The .... teller told me my future.

4 She bought a .... of flowers for her mother.

5 I don't .... her because she often doesn't tell the truth.

6 He wants to .... his girlfriend from University.

(crossword: 2 across = F I S H)

Grammar

2 Read. Then write the questions and answers for Olga and her friend Peter.

Girls

You'll be very lucky this year. You'll have very good marks at school and you'll meet a handsome boy. You will travel a lot and make a lot of new friends. You won't be rich but you'll live a long and interesting life.

Boys

You are clever and many people will like you. Be careful! You won't always be lucky. You'll live in many countries and you'll be poor sometimes. You'll marry a famous person and have two children. Your children will be very rich.

1 Olga / have a good year
Will Olga have a good year?
Yes, she will.

2 Olga / be a good pupil this year
.... ?
....

3 Olga / have a lot of money
.... ?
....

4 Olga / travel a lot
.... ?
....

5 How many children / Peter / have
.... ?
....

6 many people / like / Peter
.... ?
....

7 Peter / live in one country
.... ?
....

8 Who / Peter / marry
.... ?
....

3 Complete. Use the correct form of *will* and the verbs in brackets.

Madame Rosa You (have) ¹..will have.. a long and happy life. Your wife (love) ²................ you very much.

Clueless (be) ³................ she .... a doctor?

Madame Rosa No, she won't. She (be) ⁴................ a detective.

Clueless Where (live) ⁵................ we .... ?

Madame Rosa I don't know. But you (not / live) ⁶................ in England.

Clueless And today? What (do) ⁷................ I .... today?

Madame Rosa You (give) ⁸................ an old lady lots of money. That's £20 please!

Use your English

4 Circle the correct words.

Mrs Smith I don't usually believe ¹*in* / *at* these things. Can you really tell me about the ²*future* / *fortune*?

Madame Rosa Of course, I can!

Mrs Smith OK, let's see. What ³*do* / *will* I do tomorrow?

Madame Rosa You will ⁴*clean* / *cleaning* a big house.

Mrs Smith Correct. And next week?

Madame Rosa Next week you will ⁵*made* / *make* a wonderful cake.

Mrs Smith That's true too. Will the detectives like it?

Madame Rosa No, they ⁶*don't* / *won't*.

Mrs Smith You're wrong! You don't know the future! The detectives always like my cakes!

15 Friends' Club

Language Diary

1 I can match these adjectives with the correct prepositions and write my own examples.

1	interested	b	**a**	of	
2	fond / scared	☐	**b**	in	
3	crazy	☐	**c**	with	
4	bored	☐	**d**	at	
5	bad / good	☐	**e**	on	
6	keen	☐	**f**	about	

1 *I'm interested in the history of my country.*
2 ....
3 ....
4 ....
5 ....
6 ....

2 I know these words:

computer
website
email
mouse
mouse button

screen
keyboard
connect
click

Vocabulary

1 Label the picture.

1 *computer*   3 ....   5 ....
2 ....   4 ....

2 Look at the picture in Exercise 1. Put the letters in the correct order.

Boy Look, this computer has got a really big **ecersn** ¹*screen*..... .

Girl Yes, and the mouse has got three **tsontub** ²............. on it.

Boy That's right! Let's **nectcon** ³............. to the Internet. Now, **cckil** ⁴............. on that button.

Girl Oh, there's the *Friends' Club* **stiebew** ⁵............. on the screen. Let's write an **miale** ⁶............ to the *Friends' Club*.

Boy Great idea!

Grammar

3 Match.

1 She's very interested ☐ d
2 My brother is crazy ☐
3 We are bad ☐
4 He isn't very fond ☐
5 I'm bored ☐
6 I'm not very keen ☐

a about playing computer games.
b on Computer Studies.
c of pop music.
d in drawing.
e with television.
f at singing.

4 Circle the correct words.

Hi!

We are very ¹(*keen*)/ *crazy* on learning about you – the members of the *Friends' Club*. We are ²*fond* / *interested* in finding out about your schools, friends, families and hobbies. Please write to us! We want to know all about you! We'll never be ³*bored* / *bad* with your emails and letters.

We also want all the members to become friends. Many of our members are ⁴*good* / *crazy* at using computers and can send emails to their friends around the world – and they write them in English! Don't be ⁵*fond* / *scared* of making mistakes – write to the *Friends' Club* and make new friends!

Ally and Alex

5 Complete the sentences. Use adjectives with prepositions.

1 My class *is interested in the 'Friends' Club' magazine.*

2 My English teacher ....
....

3 My best friend ....
....

4 Many of the boys in my class ....
....

5 Many of the girls in my class ....
....

6 I ....
....

Use your English

6 Complete. Use one word in each gap.

New ▾		
Outbox		
To		Subject

From: Sandro Russo

To: Alex and Ally

Subject: Hot springs, volcanoes and earthquakes

Hi,

I'm from Curitiba in Brazil and I'm thirteen. I was very ¹*interested* in *Friends' Club* magazine this week. I'm not very ² .... on Geography but I loved reading about Greece and Iceland.

We also have earthquakes in Brazil. We are ³ .... of them. There aren't hot springs in Brazil but we can swim in the Atlantic Ocean. My best friends and I are very ⁴ .... of swimming.

I'm ⁵ .... about taking photos and I'm very ⁶ .... at it so I'm going to send some photos of Brazil to the *Friends' Club* soon.

Sandro

16 Story Time

Language Diary

1 I can complete the table.

General questions	Wh- questions
1 _Do_. you often go to the seaside?	**1** _Whose_. pen is it?
2 ...... she sometimes call you?	**2** .... many rooms are there in your house?
3 ...... you listening to music now?	**3** ....'s the title of your favourite book?
4 ...... you go camping last summer?	**4** ....'s the author of this book?
5 ...... he going to be an astronaut?	**5** .... are you now?
6 ...... you at school yesterday?	**6** .... are you scared of swimming?
7 ...... there a cinema here in 1960?	**7** .... is your birthday?

2 I know these words and expressions:

space	crash
spaceship	take off
astronaut	disappear
comet	lose contact
star	arrive
planet	travel (v)

Vocabulary

1 Match.

1. The spaceship travelled to Mars. | e |
2. It took off for Earth. | |
3. It disappeared from the screen. | |
4. It lost contact with the space station. | |
5. It crashed into the planet. | |
6. It arrived at the space station. | |

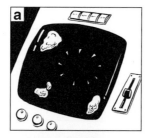

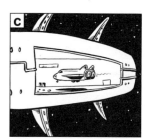

2 Complete. Use the words in the box.

> astronaut   stars   planet   spaceship
> ~~space~~   comet

I like reading stories about ¹..space.. travel
and I'm crazy about looking at the ²............
in the night sky. Sometimes I see a ³............ ,
with a long bright tail. I want to be an
⁴............ and travel in space in a ⁵............ .
I want to go to Mars, my favourite ⁶............ .

Grammar

3 Complete. Use the words in the box.

> How   What   Where   Who   Whose   ~~Which~~

1 ..Which.. planet is it?

2 .... are we going?

3 ....'s the problem?

4 **A** .... spaceship is that?

   B It's Azdie's.

5 ....'s Azdie?

6 .... many spaceships have they got?

4 Complete. Write short answers.

Joe   Did you lose contact with
           Spaceship Zeus?

Commander Yes, ¹..we did.. . But we don't
           know why.

Joe   Did Spaceship Zeus crash?

Commander No, ²............... . It disappeared.

Joe   Were there only two people in
           the spaceship?

Commander Yes, ³............... .

Dan   Are we going to take off tomorrow?

Joe   Yes, ⁴............... – at six o'clock in the
           morning.

Dan   Is the commander going to send other
           spaceships to Mars?

Joe   No, ⁵............... .

Dan   Will they have information about
           Spaceship Zeus on Mars?

Joe   Yes, ⁶............... . I'm sure.

5 Write the questions.

1 **The commander** is talking to Joe and Dan
now.
..Who is talking to Joe and Dan now?......

2 Spaceship Zeus took off for Mars **last week**.
....?

3 Dan and Joe are going to fly **to Mars**
tomorrow.
....?

4 Dan and Joe will try to find **Spaceship
Zeus**.
....?

5 **A hundred** astronauts work at the Earth
space station.
....?

6 Dan shouted **because he saw a bright light.**
....?

7 This is **Joe and Dan's** spaceship.
....?

Use your English

6 Circle the correct answer – A, B or C.

The spaceship took ¹............ from the space
station but there was a problem.

Dan   We lost ²............ with the Earth space
           station five minutes ago!

Joe   ³............ are we now?

Dan   I don't know because the ⁴............
           aren't working well. I think we're near
           Mars.

Joe   Spaceship Zeus ⁵............ near Mars!

Dan   ⁶............ are we going to do?

Joe   We must go back to Earth.

1 **A** on	**B** (off)	**C** at
2 **A** contact	**B** controls	**C** control
3 **A** Why	**B** What	**C** Where
4 **A** contact	**B** controls	**C** control
5 **A** disappeared	**B** arrived	**C** lost
6 **A** Where	**B** When	**C** What

Check Yourself
Units 13 – 16

Vocabulary

1 Put the words in the correct groups.

> ~~website~~ comet bossy hopeless
> disappear amazing fisherman arrive
> believe husband crazy

nouns	adjectives	verbs
website		

Total [5]

2 Complete. Use the words in the box.

> ~~cloakroom~~ queue emails bunch
> space cold

0 Let's put our coats in the ....cloakroom...... .

1 In the future people will travel in .... for their holidays.

2 There was a long .... for tickets.

3 My mum bought a big .... of flowers at the market.

4 I was out in the rain for two hours and I caught a ....

5 She's got a new computer and can send .... to her friends around the world.

Total [5]

Grammar

3 Complete. Use the correct form of *have to*.

0 She ...has to.. clean her room on Fridays.

1 You (not) .... believe her story.

2 I .... stay at home with my baby brother tonight.

3 .... you .... shout? I can't hear the television.

4 He (not) .... get up early on Sundays.

5 They (not) .... help in the house every day.

Total [5]

4 Complete. Use the correct form of *will* and the verbs in the box.

> ~~go out~~ connect lose marry arrive
> travel

0 I (not) ..won't go out.. tonight.

1 I .... at London at six o'clock.

2 She (not) .... her computer to the Internet tonight.

3 He .... all around the world.

4 .... I .... a famous person?

5 You .... never .... contact with real friends.

Total [10]

5 Complete. Use the correct prepositions.

0 She's very keen ....on..... animals.

1 He's very fond .... his new bike.

2 They're crazy .... sweets.

3 He's bored .... his hobby.

4 Helen isn't very good .... swimming.

5 George isn't interested .... history.

Total [5]

6 Write the questions.

0 Whose ticket is it?
....
It's **my** ticket.

1 ....
Kate will marry John **next year**.

2 ....
His dad's writing **an email**.

3 ....
The spaceship is going to crash **into the Moon**.

4 ....
He laughed **because** his friend didn't catch any fish.

5 ....
There were **five** earthquakes last year.

Total [10]

Vocabulary	[10]	Total	[40]
Grammar	[30]		

Skills Corner 4

1 Read the emails and circle the correct subjects.

1

> New ▼
> **Outbox**
> ✉ ☀ ! 📎 To | Subject
>
> **From:** Elena
>
> **Subject:** a London
> (b) The Natural History Museum
> c Dinosaurs
>
> Hi,
>
> Last year I went on holiday to London and I visited the Natural History Museum a lot. I'm not usually very keen on museums but I loved it. There were models of dinosaurs there and they were the size of real dinosaurs! Our hotel was near the museum and I spent most afternoons there. Do you like going to museums?
>
> Elena

2

> New ▼
> **Outbox**
> ✉ ☀ ! 📎 To | Subject
>
> **From:** Hasan
>
> **Subject:** a Basketball
> b English lessons
> c My school
>
> Hello!
>
> I go to a high school called Anatolian Lycee. It's a big school in the centre of Istanbul and I have to go there by bus. We have English lessons every day and we have to study other subjects in English. I'm good at English but my favourite subject is Maths. I also like sport. Next year I'll be in the school basketball team. Please tell me about your school.
>
> Hasan

3

> New ▼
> **Outbox**
> ✉ ☀ ! 📎 To | Subject
>
> **From:** Hugo
>
> **Subject:** a Tourist school
> b Languages
> c Future plans
>
> Hi,
>
> I'm going to leave school next year and then I will go to a Tourist School. It will be fun to work with tourists because I'm keen on meeting new people. Also I want to travel to other countries because I'm good at languages. Then I think I'll work in a hotel or I'll open a restaurant. What do you want to do in the future?
>
> Hugo

2 Read the notes about Pierre. Who is the best email friend for him: Elena, Hasan or Hugo? Why?

- goes to school in France
- interested in History / languages / learning about the world
- likes travelling and visiting different places
- very fond of animals / has got a dog

3 Write an email from Pierre to his new email friend in your notebook.

> New ▼
> **Outbox**
> ✉ ☀ ! 📎 To | Subject
>
> **To:** ....
>
> **From:** Pierre
>
> **Subject:** ....
>
> Hi,
>
> I was very interested in your email …
>
> ....

4 Choose the best email friend for you. Write an email to him / her in your notebook.

> New ▼
> **Outbox**
> ✉ ☀ ! 📎 To | Subject
>
> **To:** ....
>
> **From:** ....
>
> **Subject:** ....
>
> Hi,
>
> My name's … and I'm from …
>
> ....

Language Diary

① I can write my own examples.

② I know these words:

Present Perfect	Examples
positive	He has brought a stray cat to the RSPCA.
	1 I have ....
	2 ....
negative	Vicki hasn't talked to the vet.
	3 ....
	4 ....
questions	Have you met my friend?
	5 ....
	6 ....

stray
cruel
cruelty
volunteer (n)
owner
vet
injection
puppy
organisation
feed

Vocabulary

1 Complete. Use the words in the box.

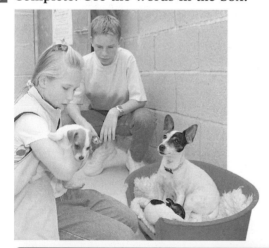

volunteers ~~owners~~ stray cruel
organisations

Most ¹.owners. are very kind to their pets but some people are ².......... to animals. Several ³.......... look after hurt or lost animals – the RSPCA is the most famous. It tries to find new homes for ⁴.......... cats and dogs. Some animal lovers work at RSPCA as ⁵.......... .

2 Find four more words in the word snake. Then complete the sentences.

1 My cat is very ill and needs an ....
2 I have to .... my dog two times a day.
3 My friend wants to be a .... and work in an animal clinic.
4 A young dog is called a ....
5 The RSPCA tries to stop .cruelty. to animals.

Grammar

3 Complete. Use the Present Perfect.

Mark (be) ¹ *has been* to the RSPCA lots of times because he loves animals. He (find) ² .... two stray cats and he (take) ³ .... them there. Now these cats (have) ⁴ .... their injections and are ready to go to new homes.

4 Write the questions. Use the Present Perfect. Then complete the answers.

1 Bob / brush / all the dogs at the RSPCA
Has Bob brushed all the dogs at the RSPCA?
Yes, *he has.*

2 Bob / feed / all the cats
.... ?
No, ...

3 Vicki / choose / a puppy
.... ?
Yes, ...

4 Vicki's puppy / have / its injections
.... ?
Yes, ...

5 Vicki / speak / to the vet
.... ?
No, ...

6 Mark / see / Mickey the monkey
.... ?
No, ...

5 Complete. Use the Past Simple or the Present Perfect.

Vicki (find) ¹ *Has* the RSPCA *found* lots of stray dogs this year in our town?

Bob Yes, it has. It (find) ² *found* twenty last month.

Bob (bring) ³ .... you .... any stray animals to the RSPCA, Mark?

Mark Yes, I have. I (bring) ⁴ .... two stray cats last week.

Bob Did you? What colour were they?

Kim (see) ⁵ .... you .... Vicki's new puppy, Rob?

Rob No, I haven't. (choose) ⁶ .... she .... a name for him?

Kim No, she hasn't. His name's Lucky. The RSPCA (choose) ⁷ .... his name when he was born there.

Use your English

6 Circle the correct answer – A, B or C.

Rob Hello! Do you work here?

Kelly Yes, I do. I'm a new ¹ .... here. ² .... you been to the RSPCA before?

Rob Yes, I have. Lots of times.

Kelly What's wrong with your dog? Is he ³ ....

Rob No, he's fine. I've ⁴ .... him here to see the vet because he has to have his ⁵ ....

Kelly Yes, it's important to keep a dog healthy. What's his name?

Rob Rex. I ⁶ .... him from the RSPCA two years ago.

1	A volunteer	B owner	C friend
2	A Has	B Have	C Did
3	A cruel	B stray	C hurt
4	A brought	B bring	C bringing
5	A prevention	B organisation	C injection
6	A have taken	B took	C has taken

43

18 Crazy Detectives

Language Diary

1 I can write my own examples.

Present Perfect: ever, never	Examples
ever	Have you ever eaten snails? **1** Has she ever ... ? **2** .... ?
never	She's never been to England. **3** .... **4** ....

2 I know these words:

dangerous   fly
disgusting   win
perfect   prize

Vocabulary

1 Complete. Use the words in the box.

> ~~prize~~   perfect   dangerous   fly
> disgusting   win

1 What was the ..prize.. in the 'Know your friend' show?

2 Did the detectives .... the holiday in Japan?

3 Clueless wants to .... in a hot-air balloon.

4 Holmes doesn't speak Japanese but her French is ....

5 The detectives aren't safe. They have a .... job.

6 Holmes has never eaten snails. She thinks they are ....

Grammar

2 Write the sentences. Use the Present Perfect and *never*.

1 eat snails

Holmes has never eaten snails.

2 fly in a hot-air balloon

....

3 see a ghost

....

4 fly in a plane

....

5 have an injection

....

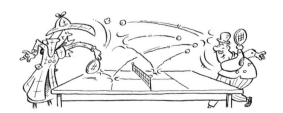

6 play table tennis

....

3 Put the words in the correct order to make questions. Then answer the questions.

1 a famous person ever have met you

Have you ever met a famous person?

Yes, I have. / No, I haven't

2 your family ever had a dog has

.... ?

....

3 your grandparents have ever
to another country been

.... ?

....

4 your favourite pop star
met have ever you

.... ?

....

5 a stray dog ever found have you

.... ?

....

6 ever your class a prize won has

.... ?

....

Use your English

4 Circle the correct words.

Clueless Have you ¹never / *ever* been to
this restaurant before?

Holmes Yes, I ²have / did. It's my
favourite restaurant. The food is
³dangerous / delicious here.

Clueless Have they got snails here?

Holmes Yes, they have. But I've ⁴never /
ever eaten them. I think they're
⁵perfect / disgusting.

Clueless Have they got ⁶Japanese / Japan
food?

Holmes Yes, they have. Why?

Clueless I've never had it and I want to
try it before our holiday.

45

19 Friends' Club

Language Diary

1 I can write my own examples.

Present Perfect: *just, yet*	Examples
positive	She has just bought her swimming costume. **1** I've just ....
negative	We haven't bought the plane tickets yet. **2** ....
questions	Have you seen Tom's girlfriend yet? **3** ....

2 I know these words:

octopus	sharp
shark	huge
dolphin	rough
seal	smooth
crab	thick
whale	romantic

Vocabulary

1 Complete. Use the adjectives in the box.

> ~~smooth~~   huge   rough   thick
> romantic   sharp

1 It's nice to touch a baby's skin because it's very ...smooth.. .

2 My boyfriend bought a bunch of flowers for me. He is so ....

3 Be careful! This knife is very ....

4 I have .... skin on my hands – I must use some cream.

5 Dinosaurs were .... animals. Some were over thirty metres tall!

6 That book is very .... – it's got 700 pages.

2 Complete.

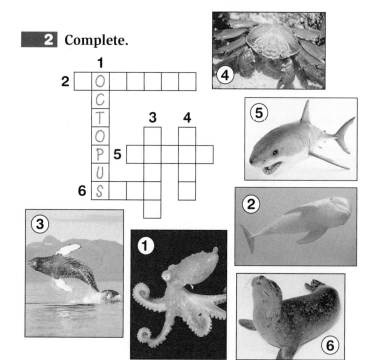

46

Grammar

3 Match the sentences with the pictures.

1 We haven't seen that film yet.

2 We've just seen that film.

3 I haven't finished my homework yet.

4 I've just finished my homework.

5 I haven't had my breakfast yet.

6 I've just had my breakfast.

A 1

B

C

D

E

F

4 Write the questions and answers.

> Alex, please visit the photographer. ✓
>
> Ally, buy a book on whales, please. ✗
>
> Alex and Ally, please answer the letter to the magazine. ✗
>
> Alex, please take the recording of the whale song to Room 1. ✓

1 Alex

Has Alex visited the photographer yet?
Yes, he's just visited him.

2 Ally

.... ?

....

3 Alex and Ally

.... ?

....

4 Alex

.... ?

....

Use your English

5 Circle the correct words.

Dad How are Sophie and Pascal?

Mum They're fine. They've ¹*just* / *yet* bought their swimming things but they haven't had their injections yet.

Dad ²*Have* / *Did* they bought a camera yet?

Mum No, ³*not yet* / *not now*. Have you seen any humpback whales ⁴*yet* / *just*?

Dad Yes, I have. They're beautiful.

Mum You're lucky. I've ⁵*never* / *yet* seen a whale.

Dad I've ⁶*just* / *never* sent Pascal and Sophie some photos of them. Have you bought your plane tickets yet?

Mum Yes, we have. See you next week!

20 Story Time

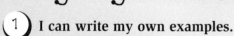

Language Diary

1 I can write my own examples.

some-, any-, no-	Examples	
somebody	1	Somebody stole my bag...
something	2	....
somewhere	3	....
anybody	4	I haven't ....
	5	Have you .... ?
anything	6	....
	7	.... ?
anywhere	8	....
	9	.... ?
nobody	10	....
nothing	11	....
nowhere	12	....

2 I know these words:

conquer
capture
throw
shine
tie
ruler
guard
alarm

Vocabulary

1 Complete. Use the words in the box.

> capture ~~ruler~~ conquer throw shine
> guards tie

Azdie is the ¹ruler........ of Planet Kitra. Her
yellow eyes ²................ in the dark. Azdie
has a plan to ³................ Dan and Joe and
⁴................ the Earth. Azdie's ⁵................
have put the astronauts in the conversion
room. She wants to change the astronauts into
Kitrans. But Joe and Dan have escaped from
the conversion room. They decided to
⁶................ a jacket over Azdie's head and
⁷................ her to a chair.

Grammar

2 Complete. Use *some-, any-, no-*.

Joe I can hear a voice. Is there ¹ *anybody* outside the door?

Dan Yes, there is. I think it's a guard.

Joe What's he doing?

Dan ² .... , he's only standing there. But I think he's talking to ³ .... on a telephone system now.

Joe I can see ⁴ .... outside the window. It's big and black but it isn't our spaceship.

Dan Yes, they've moved our spaceship ⁵ ....

Joe How will we find it?

Dan I don't know. But at the moment there's ⁶ .... we can do about it.

3 Circle the correct words.

1 I've just heard *anything /* (*something*) strange.

2 I can't see *anybody / nobody*.

3 Please don't say *something / anything* to the guards.

4 Have you seen *anybody / nobody* from planet Kitra?

5 *Nobody / Anybody* has been in this room today.

6 *Nothing / Anything* will stop Azdie now!

4 Complete the dialogues. Use *some-, any-, no-*.

1 Guard 1 Are you going to do *anything* tonight?

Guard 2 No, I'm not. I'm very tired.

2 Guard 1 What have you eaten today?

Guard 2 .... so I'm very hungry. I must have some dinner soon!

3 Guard 1 Have you ever seen .... from the Moon?

Guard 2 Never! What are they like?

4 Guard 1 Where are you going for your holiday?

Guard 2 .... I'm going to stay here.

5 Guard 1 Have the astronauts eaten .... today?

Guard 2 No, they haven't. We must give them .... to eat.

5 Answer the questions.

1 Have you been anywhere interesting this week?
   No, I haven't. / Yes, I've been to ....

2 Is there anybody in the room with you at the moment?
   ....

3 Do you know anybody from Australia?
   ....

4 Do you want to go anywhere with your friends this evening?
   ....

5 Are you going to eat anything special this evening?
   ....

Use your English

6 Rewrite the sentences. Use the words in CAPITALS.

1 The spaceship isn't anywhere   NOWHERE
   near the space station.
   The spaceship is nowhere near the
   space station.

2 I'm hungry but there's   ANYTHING
   nothing to eat.
   ....

3 The astronauts can go   ANYWHERE
   nowhere without their spaceship.
   ....

4 We can't do anything now   NOTHING
   because they're watching us.
   ....

5 We have seen nobody   ANYBODY
   from Kitra!
   .... !

6 People on Earth don't know   NOTHING
   anything about Azdie's plan.
   ....

49

Check Yourself
Units 17 – 20

Vocabulary

1 Put the words in the correct groups.

> octopus puppy owner guard vet
> volunteer shark crab ruler seal
> whale

person	animal
	octopus

Total ☐ 5

2 Match the opposites.

0 correct	d	**a** delicious
1 dangerous	☐	**b** rough
2 disgusting	☐	**c** little
3 huge	☐	**d** wrong
4 thick	☐	**e** safe
5 smooth	☐	**f** thin

Total ☐ 5

Grammar

3 Complete the dialogues. Use the Past Simple or the Present Perfect.

A (meet) ⁰ Have you met our new teacher?
B Yes, I have. I (meet) ⁰ met her yesterday.

A (clean) ¹.......... Kate .... her bedroom?
B Yes, she has. She (clean) ².......... it last night.

A When (feed) ³.......... you .... the cat?
B I (feed) ⁴.......... it last night.

A You (not / brush) ⁵.......... your hair!
B Yes, I have! I (brush) ⁶.......... it five minutes ago.

Total ☐ 12

4 Complete.

Infinitive	Past Participle
0 fly	flown
1 eat	....
2 catch	....
3 win	....
4 know	....
5 be	....

Total ☐ 5

5 Complete the dialogues. Use *just*, *yet*, *ever* or *never*.

A Have you ⁰ ever seen a shark?
B No, ¹.......... ! Have you?
A No, not ².......... . But I think I will on my holiday.

A I've ³.......... watched 'The Lost Spaceship'.
B Oh, I haven't seen it ⁴.......... . Is it good?
A It's great! I've ⁵.......... seen a better film!

A I've ⁶.......... come back from my holiday.
B You're lucky! I haven't had my holiday ⁷.......... . Where did you go?
A I went to France. Have you ⁸.......... been to France?

Total ☐ 8

6 Complete. Use *some-*, *any-* or *no-*.

0 I think some thing strange has happened in this house.
1 Did ....body hear the alarm last night?
2 Have you seen my puppy ....where?
3 ....body likes her new book because it's boring.
4 I slept all day and did ....thing.
5 Where's Tom? Has ....body seen him?

Total ☐ 5

Vocabulary	☐ 10
Grammar	☐ 30
Total	☐ 40

Skills Corner 5

1 **Read. Then match the questions with the paragraphs.**

1 What does the word *hippo* mean?   `a`

2 What are tusks?   ☐

3 What do hippos and elephants eat?   ☐

4 How heavy are elephants?   ☐

5 What can elephants do with their trunks?   ☐

6 What do angry hippos do?   ☐

Two Big <u>Animals from Africa!</u>

b

Hippos are about one and a half metres tall. One hippo weighs about the same as 120 eight-year-old children! They are dark grey. Their skin is smooth with some hair on it. They've got small ears and eyes but their mouths are huge. Angry hippos always open their mouths!

c

African elephants are the biggest land animals. One elephant is usually heavier than six cars. Elephants have got rough, thick skin, small eyes and huge ears. They also have a very long nose, called a trunk. Elephants can smell, touch and pick up very heavy things with their trunks!

a

Elephants and hippos are among the biggest animals in Africa. Hippo is a short word for hippopotamus and it means *river horse*. Hippos are called *river horses* because they live in rivers and lakes and eat grass. Elephants live on the land but they like spending time in rivers and lakes. They throw water over their bodies in very hot weather. They eat a lot of grass too.

d

Elephants and hippos have got tusks. Hippos' tusks are usually about half a metre long but elephants' tusks are much longer. Tusks are teeth but these animals don't use them for eating. They fight other animals with them!

Writing

2a **Look at the picture of rhinoceroses and read the notes about them.**

- live in Asia
- usually called 'rhinos' for short
- rhinoceros means nose-horn
- have got two horns
- are about 1.5 metre high and 3 metres long
- have got hair on their bodies
- eat grass and fruit
- like lying in water and mud

2b **Write a description of rhinoceroses. Use the adjectives in the box. Look at the picture and use the notes in Exercise 2a and your own ideas.**

| huge   long   short   hairy   thick   rough |

Rhinoceroses live in Asia. They're called 'rhinos' for short.

....

....

....

....

....

....

....

21 The LONDONERS

Language Diary

1 **I can write my own examples.**

can, could (requests)

Could you open the window, please?

1 ....

can, could (permissions)

Can I sit here?

2 ....

Would you like ... ? (offers)

Would you like a sandwich?

3 ....

2 **I know these words:**

theatre	interval
audience	programme
stage	comedy
actor	clap

Vocabulary

1 **Match.**

1 A break in the middle of the play. `f`

2 We watch plays in this building. ☐

3 These people watch a play. ☐

4 This man acts in plays and films. ☐

5 People act on this. ☐

6 We do this at the end of a good play. ☐

7 You can find information about the play in this. ☐

8 People laugh a lot when they watch it. ☐

a programme
b comedy
c theatre
d actor
e stage
f interval
g clap
h audience

Grammar

2 Circle the correct words.

1 (Could) / Would I have an ice cream, please?

2 Could / Would you like a sandwich?

3 Can / Would I use your umbrella, Vicki?

4 Would / Could anybody like a drink?

5 Could / Would I open the window, Mr Grant?

6 Can / Would you like a programme?

3 Complete. Use *can* / *could* or *would*.

1 ..Could.. we watch television, please?

2 .... I carry these bags for you?

3 .... you like a drink?

4 .... I go and get a drink, please?

5 .... you help, please?

Use your English

4 Circle the correct words.

Mr Grant Did you enjoy the [1](play) / stage last night?

Kim Yes, I did. The king was my favourite [2]audience / actor.

Mark There is a photo of him in the [3]interval / programme. [4]Would / Can you like it?

Kim Oh, thanks, Mark.

Rob [5]Could / Would we go to the theatre again?

Mr Grant Certainly. But now [6]can't / can you open your books at page ten, please? We're going to talk about Shakespeare today.

22 Crazy Detectives

Language Diary

1 I can write my own examples.

adjective + preposition + *ing* / *nouns*: questions

good at	**crazy about**
What are you good at?	.... ?
Is she good at swimming?	.... ?

bad at	**keen on**
.... ?	.... ?
.... ?	.... ?

interested in	**fond of**
.... ?	.... ?
.... ?	.... ?

2 I know these words and expressions:

horse riding	cooking
judo	collecting stamps
chess	take up
cards	collect
gardening	collection

Vocabulary

1 Circle the correct words.

1 My hobby is (cooking) / *collecting* because I love good food.

2 *Gardening / Chess* is my favourite game.

3 My uncle has got a big stamp *collection / collecting*.

4 Animal lovers often choose *judo / horse riding* as a hobby.

5 *Judo / Cards* is a great sport.

6 My grandfather wants to *collect / take up* a new hobby.

Grammar

2 Complete and answer the questions.

1 Are you interested ...in.. taking up a hobby?
Yes, I am. / No, I'm not ....

2 What sport are you good ...... ?
....

3 Who are you fond ...... at your school?
....

4 Which school subjects are you interested ...... ?
....

5 Is your best friend keen ...... playing chess?
....

6 What animals are you scared ...... ?
....

3 Put the words in the correct order to make questions. Then answer the questions.

1 | Holmes | what | is | at | good |

What is Holmes
good at?
She's good at playing
the violin.

2 | good | is | what | at | Mrs Smith |

....
.... ?
....
....

3 | keen | what | Clueless | is | on |

....
.... ?
....

4 | very | who | of | Mrs Smith | is | fond |

....
.... ?
....
....

5 | about | Clueless | what | is | crazy |

....
.... ?
....
....

4 Complete. Use sentences a–e.

Interviewer	Now, you play the violin, Ms Holmes.
Holmes	Yes, but I'm bored with the violin. ¹I want to take up another hobby.
Interviewer	Well, are you interested in sport?
Holmes	Yes, ²............................ .
Interviewer	And what sport are you good at?
Holmes	³.............. But I don't want to take up a sport.
Interviewer	Are you keen on collecting things?
Holmes	⁴................................... .
Interviewer	Are you fond of games?
Holmes	⁵................................. .
Interviewer	Then you can take up chess!
Holmes	A great idea but I play chess every day and I'm bored with it.

a Well, I'm good at playing them.
b I'm not bad at running and swimming.
c I'm keen on sport.
d I want to take up another hobby.
e Well, not really. I don't want to start a collection.

Use your English

5 Rewrite the sentences. Use the words in CAPITALS.

1 The detectives like dancing. FOND OF
The detectives are fond of dancing.

2 Mrs Smith wants to   INTERESTED IN
know everything
about judo.
....

3 Holmes is a good violin   GOOD AT
player.
....

4 Clueless isn't a good singer.   BAD AT
....

5 Holmes loves   CRAZY ABOUT
swimming.
....

6 Mrs Smith thinks   BORED WITH
detective stories
are boring.
....

23 Friends' Club

Language Diary

1 I can write my own examples.

should / shouldn't	Examples
positive	You should be nice to your friends. 1 ....
negative	You shouldn't worry about clothes. 2 ....
questions	Should I talk to my teacher about it? 3 ....

2 I know these words and expressions:

free time	explain
on time	quarrel (v)
all the time	be proud of
a long time	organise
a good time	

Vocabulary

1 Complete. Use the expressions in the box.

> a long time   all the time   a good time
> free time   on time

1 He doesn't have his swimming lessons this week so he will have more ...free time...... .

2 I spent .... on my homework last night.

3 The train left .... but it arrived ten minutes late.

4 We had .... on holiday because the weather was great.

5 We have to wear school uniforms at school but at home I wear jeans ....

2 Replace the underlined words with the words in the box.

> quarrel   ~~organise~~   was proud of   explain

1 Why don't you **plan** your free time?
...organise.....................

2 Harry did some good work and he **felt good about** it.

....

3 Why do you always **fight** with your brother?

....

4 The teacher didn't **tell us everything about** the new project yesterday.

....

Grammar

3 Complete. Use *should* or *shouldn't*.

1 Children ...should... go to bed early.

2 You .... quarrel with your friends.

3 We .... eat a lot of fruit. It's very good for us.

4 Nobody .... eat a lot of sweets. They're bad for our teeth.

5 You .... learn to ride a bike. It's great fun.

6 We .... be late for school.

7 I think all schools .... have an indoor swimming pool!

4 Give advice. Use *should* and *shouldn't*.

1 I want to be good at English.
 You should study every day.
 You shouldn't use your own language in
 English classes.

2 She wants to be thinner.
 ....
 ....
 ....

3 They want to go to Italy for a holiday but haven't got a lot of money.
 ....
 ....
 ....

4 He's keen on finding a new pen friend.
 ....
 ....
 ....

5 She doesn't have any free time on Sundays.
 ....
 ....
 ....

6 She's often late for school.
 ....
 ....
 ....

5 Read Sue's letter and give her your own advice. Write five sentences.

Dear Alex and Ally,

All my friends like pop music and discos, but I don't. I think pop music is terrible and I've never been to a disco because I think I'm very bad at dancing. I like classical music and often go concerts. I've got a lot of CDs with classical music at home and I love listening to them. Some of my friends laugh at me. But they have never listened to classical music or been to an opera. What should I do?

Sue

1 ....
 ....

2 ....
 ....

3 ....
 ....

4 ....
 ....

5 ....
 ....

Use your English

6 Complete. Use one word in each gap.

I go to school by bus every day. I'm always [1]...on.... time for the bus [2]............ it is often late. Then of course I'm late [3].......... school and I don't have time [4]............ finish my homework before lessons. What should I do?

Jane

Ally's advice

I think you should finish your homework [5]............ the evening. You shouldn't do it in the morning! And I think you [6].......... catch an earlier bus.

24 Story Time

Language Diary

1 **I can write my own examples.**

Suggestions

Let's have a party!

1 .....Lets..this afternoon..

Let's not talk about it now!

2 ....

What about using this machine?

3 ....

Why don't we use the transporter?

4 ....

2 **I know these words:**

scientist   escape (v)
tunnel   return (v)
sunglasses   destroy
machine

Vocabulary

1 **Put the letters in the correct order. Then find them in the word square. Look → ↓.**

1 The astronauts saw a strange **ceinmha**
   .machine. outside the conversion room.

2 Joe and Dan left the conversion room and went into a dark **nunlte** ....

3 **essticsnti** .... on Earth made the first transporter.

4 Are the Kitrans going to **stoeyrd** .... Joe and Dan's spaceship?

5 Dan and Joe wanted to **pcaese** .... from Kitra and **tenurr** .... home.

6 The commander took off his **ulsgassens** .... and Dan and Joe saw his yellow eyes!

s	c	i	e	n	t	i	s	t	s
d	u	r	e	t	a	s	s	y	a
e	d	e	s	c	a	p	e	r	e
s	u	n	g	l	a	s	s	e	s
t	m	a	c	h	h	n	e	t	n
r	e	t	u	n	n	e	l	u	m
o	k	d	g	l	a	s	e	r	e
y	m	a	c	h	i	n	e	n	g

Grammar

2 Complete Joe's and Dan's suggestions.
Use *let's ... , why don't ... , what about ...* .

Joe ¹..l̲e̲t̲'̲s̲.. go into the tunnel! The alarm is ringing and the guards will be here soon.

Dan ².............. trying to stop the alarm? That will give us more time.

Joe No! I can see a light at the end of the tunnel. Quick, ³.............. run!

Dan The controls of this transporter are very strange.

Joe Yes, they're different from the controls in our spaceship. ⁴.............. we use other controls?

Dan OK! Great! The engines are working now. ⁵.............. trying to contact the commander?

Joe No, we haven't got time. We'll be back home in minutes.

Dan We're home. There's the commander.

Joe Does he know anything about Azdie and Planet Kitra?

Dan ⁶.............. ask him!

3 Make suggestions. Use the words in brackets.

1 You want to go out somewhere. (cinema)
What about ..g̲o̲i̲n̲g̲ ̲t̲o̲ ̲t̲h̲e̲ ̲c̲i̲n̲e̲m̲a̲?̲............

2 It's your teacher's birthday today. (flowers)
Let's ....

3 You and your friends aren't hungry. (not / eat now)
Let's ....

4 You don't want to play football. (tennis)
Why .... ?

5 It's very hot. (swimming pool)
Let's ....

6 You want to stay at home because it's very cold. (television)
What about .... ?

Use your English

4 Circle the correct words.

Dan Look, the commander's eyes are yellow! He's Kitran! We must ¹*escape* / *return* from here!

Joe What about ²*use* / *using* the transporter to go back to Kitra?

Dan No, let's ³*go* / *going* to the police and tell them about Azdie's plan.

Joe Why don't we ⁴*contact* / *contacting* the newspapers too?

Dan That's a good idea, but let's ⁵*don't* / *not* do it now. We haven't got a lot of time. The Kitrans will be here soon. ⁶*Let's* / *What about* talk to our families first.

Check Yourself

Units 21 – 24

Vocabulary

1 Circle the odd one out.

0 actor (audience) commander teacher
1 swimming dancing eating horse riding
2 chess judo horse gardening
3 stage theatre play machine
4 crazy about bored with fond of keen on
5 cheer talk organise shout

Total [ ] 5

2 Complete. Use the words in the box.

> quarrel collection ~~comedy~~ explain
> escape programme

0 We saw a very funny ..comedy. at a new open-air theatre.
1 I started my stamp .... two years ago.
2 The thief tried to .... in a car but the police caught him.
3 My sister and I don't always agree. We sometimes ....
4 I don't understand this game. Can you .... it to me please?
5 We read about the play in the ....

Total [ ] 5

Grammar

3 Complete. Use *can / could* or *would you like*.

0 ..Could... you shut the window, please?
1 I'm very hungry, Mum. .... I have a sandwich?
2 .... I use your computer?
3 .... some lemonade?
4 .... you move your bag, please?
5 .... my umbrella? I've got a raincoat.
6 .... I ride your bike?

Total [ ] 6

4 Complete. Use *let's (not)*, *what about* or *why don't*.

0 ..Why don't.. you take up horse riding?
1 .... meet tonight.
2 .... you learn to play the violin?
3 .... cooking pizza tonight?
4 .... tell her! She'll be angry.

Total [ ] 8

5 Make questions for the answers.

0 .Are you keen on gardening?...............

Yes, I'm very keen on gardening.
.What are you interseted in?..........

I'm very interested in **Biology**.

1 ....?

My friend is good at **basketball**.

2 ....?

He's very fond of **his new camera**.

3 ....?

Yes, my dad is keen on canoeing.

4 ....?

She's crazy about **pop music**.

Total [ ] 8

6 Complete. Use *should* or *shouldn't*.

Mum You 0 .shouldn't....... eat sweets, Kelly!
Kelly Why 1 .... I, Mum?
Mum Sweets are very bad for your teeth. And you 2 .... eat between meals.
Kelly But I'm always hungry.
Mum Then you 3 .... eat fruit.
Kelly But I like sweets!
Mum Then you 4 .... brush your teeth more often.

Total [ ] 8

Vocabulary	10
Grammar	30
Total	40

Skills Corner 6

Reading

1 Read and circle the correct words.

Dear Paul,

Thank you for your letter. I've told my friends about you ¹(so) / because now they all want to meet my cousin from London!

Mum wants to take us to the new open-air theatre in our town ²but / because there's a good play there next week. Do you like the theatre?

I know you're very keen on horses ³so / and what about going horse riding? I go every week ⁴but / so I'm not very good at it yet.

There's a new film at the cinema about sharks in Australia ⁵because / and all my friends say it's great. Why don't we go to see it together?

Please write soon.

Best wishes,

Tom

2 Read again and circle the correct answers.

1 Paul is Tom's cousin.

  A (right)   **B** wrong   **C** doesn't say

2 Paul has visited Tom before.

  A right   **B** wrong   **C** doesn't say

3 There's an open-air theatre in Tom's town.

  A right   **B** wrong   **C** doesn't say

4 Tom's mum doesn't want to go to the theatre.

  A right   **B** wrong   **C** doesn't say

5 Paul doesn't like horses.

  A right   **B** wrong   **C** doesn't say

6 Tom's friends like the new film about sharks.

  A right   **B** wrong   **C** doesn't say

Writing

3 Read Paul's letter and Tom's notes. Then complete Tom's reply.

Dear Tom,

Thanks for your letter. I'm going to come next Sunday. My train arrives at four p.m. Can you meet me at the station?

yes / Mum and I drive to the station

Yes, I like the theatre. I want to see the theatre in your town because I've never been to an open-air theatre! What's the title of the play? My mum wants to pay for the tickets.

title: The Happy King ! / pay for tickets – no

I've never been horse riding but I want to try! Do I have to wear special clothes? What clothes should I bring? What other things should I bring?

comfortable clothes for horse riding / bring swimming costume and roller blades

I'm sorry but I saw the film about sharks last week. It was fantastic! You should see it. What about going to see the new Harry Potter film? What other things can we do?

Harry Potter film – yes

canoeing?

See you soon!

Paul

Dear Paul,

Thanks for your letter. Of course I can meet you at the station!

....

....

....

....

....

See you soon!

Tom

26 Crazy Detectives

Language Diary

1 I can write my own examples.

> **Past Continuous:** *while, when*
>
> While she was watching TV, her sister was reading a book.
> **1** While I was ....
> ....
> They were shopping when they saw their friends.
> **2** .... when ... .

2 I know these words:

greengrocer's	purse	collect
butcher's	necklace	chase
baker's	safe (n)	earn
fishmonger's		
jeweller's		

Vocabulary

1 Write the names of the shops.

Shopping

1 fish
   fishmonger's ....

2 meat
   ....

3 bread and a chocolate cake
   ....

4 bananas
   ....

5 watch and necklace
   ....

2 Replace the underlined words. Use the words in the box.

> chase   collect   purse   ~~safe~~   earn

1 His uncle keeps his money and jewellery in a **strong box with a key**.
.safe............

2 The detectives started to **run after** the thief but he got into a car and escaped.
....

3 He's going **to go and take** his children from school.
....

4 How much money do teachers **get**?
....

5 She always carries a **little bag with her money in it**.
....

Grammar

3 Complete. Use the Past Simple or the Past Continuous.

1 While Holmes (work) <u>was working</u>., Clueless went to the shops.

2 Mrs Smith went into the jeweller's while Clueless (buy) .... bread at the baker's.

3 While Mrs Smith (shop) .... , she left her glasses in the jeweller's shop.

4 Mrs Smith was leaving the jeweller's when Clueless (see) .... her.

5 Mrs Smith was running home when Clueless (throw) .... some food at her.

6 Holmes (work) .... when Mrs Smith returned home.

4 Look at the picture and complete the sentences.

1 Holmes / play her violin / Clueless / have a bath
Holmes <u>was playing her violin</u> while <u>Clueless was having a bath</u>.

2 Who / read a book / a burglar / break the window
Who <u>was reading a book</u> when <u>a burgular broke the window</u> ?

3 Holmes / play her violin / a burglar / break into the house.
Holmes .... when ....

4 Mrs Smith / sweep the floor / she / listen to the radio
While Mrs Smith ....

5 Who / read a book / Holmes / shout 'Help!'
Who .... when .... ?

6 Mrs Smith / clean the house / the baker / knock at the door
Mrs Smith .... when ....

7 The dog / chase the cat / Mrs Smith / sweep the floor
While ....

Use your English

5 Rewrite the sentences.

1 My brother was buying vegetables. A famous footballer walked into the greengrocer's.
<u>My brother was buying vegetables when a famous footballer walked into the greengrocer's.</u> or
<u>While my brother was buying vegetables, a famous footballer walked into the greengrocer's.</u>

2 They were playing basketball in the park. It started to rain.
....

3 My friend was watching television. A police officer knocked at his door.
....

4 You were eating dinner. I was shopping.
....

5 They were playing chess. A burglar climbed through their window.
....

6 The phone rang. I was having a bath.
....

27 Friends' Club

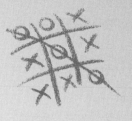

Language Diary

1 I can write my own examples.

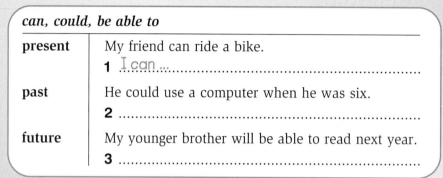

can, could, be able to	
present	My friend can ride a bike. **1** I can ....
past	He could use a computer when he was six. **2** ....
future	My younger brother will be able to read next year. **3** ....

2 I know these words:

robot	bark
brain	wag
partner	tidy (v)
pal	design (v)
	communicate

Vocabulary

1 Do the crossword.

Across:

2 The dog saw a stranger and started to ....

4 .... is another word for friend.

7 To speak or write to somebody.

8 Your room looks terrible! You must .... it before your birthday party.

9 You work, dance or play a game with this person.

Down:

1 People can think, feel, move and talk because they have got ....

3 Elsie and Elmer were the first animal ....

5 Dogs usually .... their tails when they're happy.

6 To make a drawing as a plan for something.

Grammar

2 Circle the correct words.

COMPUTERS

About four hundred years ago William Schickard, a German scientist, designed the first adding machine. It was very simple and it ¹*can't / couldn't* do many things. It ²*could / couldn't* only work with small numbers. In 1960 some scientists used Schickard's drawings and made a copy of his machine.

Today there are computers in almost every home and office. They ³*can / could* do amazing things but they ⁴*couldn't / can't* usually talk. We ⁵*can / can't* use them to communicate with people all over the world. We ⁶*could / can* play great games on them too.

I think in the future we ⁷*can / will be able to* use computers to do all our jobs.

3 Complete. Use the correct form of *can, could* or *will be able to.*

Ally What's your favourite sport?

Alex Swimming. I ¹.could... swim when I was three.

Alex How ²............. new members of the *Friends' Club* communicate with us?

Ally They ³............. write letters or use the website but they (not) ⁴............. telephone us.

Alex I've just started guitar lessons!

Ally Good, you ⁵...................... play at the next *Friends' Club* party!

Ally Why has your brother bought a new computer?

Alex Because he (not) ⁶............. play games on his old computer.

Alex ⁷............. we .... finish the newsletter tomorrow?

Ally No, we ⁸............. . I haven't got all the photos yet.

Alex Where were you at the weekend?

Ally At home. I ⁹............. go out because I was ill.

Use your English

4 Complete. Use the correct form of the words in CAPITALS.

1 My grandfather was .sixty. yesterday. — SIX

2 Dogs wag their tails to show .... — HAPPY

3 *Aibo* is a .... word. — JAPAN

4 The baby was very sweet and .... — LOVE

5 Most robots don't show their .... — FEEL

6 Many animals can't walk .... — BACK

Check Yourself
Units 25 - 28

1 **Match**

0 fish   `d`   **a** baker's

1 meat   ☐   **b** butcher's

2 necklaces   ☐   **c** greengrocer's

3 fruit and vegetables   ☐   **d** fishmonger's

4 bread   ☐   **e** jeweller's

Total   `4`

2 **Circle the correct words.**

0 I have to *dig / mow* the lawn because it has grown a lot this month.

1 Mum always *cuts / waters* the hedge very short.

2 It has been very hot today so we must *water / dig* the garden this evening.

3 We have *planted / dug* some colourful flowers in front of our house.

4 Dad *dug / planted* holes for his vegetables yesterday.

5 Do you *cut / grow* vegetables in your garden?

6 *Gardening / Watering* is a great hobby.

Total   `6`

Grammar

3 **Complete. Use the Past Continuous.**

0 I (write) .was.writing. a letter yesterday at nine o'clock.

1 (play) ...... you ...... tennis at half past five?

2 What (do) .... you .... yesterday morning at ten o'clock?

3 He (not / clean) .... his bike at five o'clock.

4 (work) .... your parents .... in the garden yesterday morning?

5 I (not / sleep) .... at eleven, I (listen) .... to the radio.

6 (do) .... she .... homework yesterday at three o'clock?

7 (watch) .... she .... TV with you at six o'clock?

Total   `8`

4 **Complete. Use the Past Simple or the Past Continuous.**

0 We (have) .were.having.. a picnic when it (start) .started. to rain.

1 While the robot (clean) .... the house, my mum (sleep) ....

2 While I (buy) .... bread, I (leave) .... my purse in the shop.

3 While he (sail) .... in the summer, he (fall) .... into the sea.

4 I (do) .... my homework when I (hear) .... a strange noise outside.

Total   `8`

5 **Complete with the correct form of *can, could* and *will be able to*.**

0 I hope I .will be able to.. speak three foreign languages in the future.

1 We (not) ...... take any photos because there was no film in the camera.

2 When she was little she (not) ...... sing but now she ...... sing and dance very well.

3 ...... people ...... build houses on other planets in the future?

Total   `4`

6 **Complete. Use the correct form of the verbs in brackets.**

One day when I (shop) **0**.was shopping... with my sister we (see) **1**.......... a robot in a toy shop. The robot (be) **2**.......... huge and it (have) **3**.......... four arms. It (can) **4**.......... walk but it (not / can) **5**.......... speak. While I (look at) **6**.......... some footballs, my sister (play) **7**.......... with the robot. Suddenly my sister (shout) **8**.......... . She (be) **9**.......... in the arms of the robot and the robot (walk) **10**.......... around the shop!

Total   `10`

Vocabulary	`10`
Grammar	`30`
Total	`40`

Skills Corner 7

Reading

1 Read and put the paragraphs in the correct order.

a ☐

I shouted at Jack but he didn't hear me. Then I started waving my bag in the air. While I was doing that, Rosie was jumping up and down and calling 'Jack! Hello, Jack!' Finally Jack heard her and started waving back to us. Then it happened!

b 1

I saw an accident today! It happened when I was walking home from school at about four o'clock. I was with my friend, Rosie. She's in my class at school.

c ☐

We were running over to the man when a car came round the corner. The car didn't hit the man but it was very frightening. The man on the bike and the driver of the car were very angry with us.

d ☐

Suddenly my school bag flew out of my hand. A man was riding a bike and the bag fell in front of him. His front wheel hit the bag and he fell off the bike.

e ☐

Rosie and I were walking down the High Street. The street was very busy. A lot of people were shopping and there was a lot of traffic. Suddenly we saw our friend Jack on the other side of the road. I was surprised to see him.

Writing

2 Read the man's notes about the accident. Write three paragraphs about the accident.

paragraph 1

cold day - April - riding my bike home from work - school children going home - a lot of traffic - many people shopping

paragraph 2

school bag flew through the air - landed in front of my bike - fell off the bike - wearing a helmet

paragraph 3

car came round the corner - shouted at the car driver - car didn't hit children - children very sorry

It was a cold day in April. I was riding ......

....

....

....

....

....

....

....

....

....

....

....

29 The LONDONERS

Language Diary

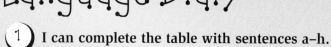

1 I can complete the table with sentences a–h.

Question tags

Positive statements

1 _Rob looks fine, doesn't he?_
2 ....
3 ....
4 ....

Negative statements

5 ....
6 ....
7 ....
8 ....

a Rob looks fine, doesn't he?
b Rob wasn't happy with his costume, was he?
c They weren't eating, were they?
d Vicki's gone to switch on the lights, hasn't she?
e You went there yesterday, didn't you?
f I'll see you soon, won't I?
g They don't have to go to school today, do they?
h You didn't tell her about it yesterday, did you?

2 I know these words:

put on	choir
speak up	concert
switch on	costume
look in	exhibition
hurry up	orchestra
take off	project

Vocabulary

1 Complete. Use the words in the box.

exhibition   choir
concert   ~~projects~~
costumes   orchestra

Last month all the pupils at our school did ¹ _projects_ about other countries. Then last week we had an International Day for the parents. There was a ².............. of music from around the world. The school ³.............. played the music and the ⁴.............. sang the songs. Some pupils wore special ⁵.............. and did dances from other countries. There was also an ⁶.............. of pupils' paintings on 'Animals Around the World'.

2 Match verbs from box A with prepositions from box B and complete the sentences.

A

speak ~~take~~ put switch hurry look

B

up (x2) ~~off~~ on (x2) in

1 You must ......take off...... your shoes because I've just swept the floor.

2 .... the light. It's dark here.

3 I can't hear you. Please ....

4 .... , we're going to be late!

5 .... your coat. It's cold outside.

6 You look very pretty in that dress. .... the mirror and you'll see!

Grammar

3 Complete. Use the correct question tags.

1 Mrs Rossi is helping Rob, ...isn't she.. ?

2 Rob looks funny in that costume, ... ?

3 Rob isn't going to put on his hat, ... ?

4 I don't have to wear that false nose, ... ?

5 Rob hasn't looked in the mirror yet, ... ?

6 Mr Grant was talking to Mrs Rossi at five, ... ?

7 Rob should go on the stage now, ... ?

4 Write the questions and answers.

1 Rob / have got / brown hair, hasn't he?
   Rob has got brown hair, hasn't he?
   Yes, he has.

2 Kim / wear / a red dress / in the play, didn't she?
   .... ?
   ....

3 Mr Grant / be / a drama teacher, isn't he?
   .... ?
   ....

4 Mr Grant / take / the Londoners / to the Globe Theatre, didn't he?
   .... ?
   ....

5 Kim and Vicki / not / be / friends / last year, were they?
   .... ?
   ....

6 You / be / in a school play, won't you?
   .... ?

5 Match.

1 Vicki doesn't have to … [c]
2 Kim couldn't … ☐
3 Mark shouldn't … ☐
4 The Londoners can … ☐
5 The children are going to … ☐
6 The parents will … ☐

a … laugh at Rob, should he?
b … have a party after the play, aren't they?
c … wear a false nose in the play, does she?
d … enjoy the play tonight, won't they?
e … find her hat before the play, could she?
f … act very well, can't they?

Use your English

6 Complete.

Mark The play was fun, [1]wasn't it?

Kim Yes. I loved wearing the Chinese costume. My princess dress [2]............. beautiful, wasn't it?

Vicki Yes, you looked pretty in it. You can wear it at next week's fancy dress party, [3]............. you?

Kim Good idea! And Rob acted very well, didn't [4]............. ?

Vicki Yes, but he took [5]............. his false nose just before he went on the stage, [6]............. he?

Mark Yes, he did!

30 Crazy Detectives

Language Diary

1 I can write my own examples.

enough, too	
enough	The cake is sweet enough. **1** ....
not enough	The tea isn't hot enough. **2** ....
too	These shoes are too big for me. **3** ....

as + adjective + as, not as + adjective + as	
as ... as	Holmes is as bad-tempered as Clueless. **4** ....
not as ... as	She isn't as tall as her friend. **5** ....

2 I know these words:

bad-tempered	polite
good-tempered	kind
easy-going	unkind
difficult	weak
rude	strong

Vocabulary

1 Write the opposites. Then complete the sentences.

a good-tempered – b <u>ad-t</u> <u>e</u> <u>m</u> <u>p</u> <u>e</u> <u>r</u> <u>e</u> d
b difficult – _ _ _ y-_ _ i _ _
c polite – _ _ _ e
d unkind – _ i _ _
e weak – _ t _ _ _ _

1 You're very .... so this box shouldn't be too heavy for you.

2 Their new teacher often shouts at his pupils. He's <u>bad-tempered</u> .

3 It is .... to help your friends.

4 My best friend is never angry or worried about anything. He's very ....

5 He is very .... because he never says 'please' or 'thank you'.

Grammar

2 Write sentences about the three dogs. Use *not as … as, as … as* and the adjectives in the box.

> tall   fat   long   nice   ~~friendly~~
> bad-tempered   pretty   short   small

| FIDO | REX | PUG |

1 *I think Pug isn't as friendly as Fido and Rex.*

2 ....
....

3 ....
....

4 ....
....

5 ....
....

6 ....
....

7 ....
....

8 ....
....

9 ....
....

3 Complete. Use *too* or *enough* and the adjectives in the box.

> fat   small   ~~strong~~   cold   long   sweet

1 Could I have some milk, please? This tea is *too strong* .

2 This tea isn't ....! Can I have some sugar, please?

3 Clueless, you must cut your hair. It's ....

4 No cake for me, thank you. I'm .... now.

5 You only need a jacket, Holmes. It isn't .... today for a coat.

6 You can't wear this hat, Holmes. It's .... for you!

4 Tick ✓ true. Cross ✗ false. Then correct the false sentences.

1 I'm as tall as my best friend. ☒
I'm not as tall as my best friend.

2 I'm as easy-going as my best friend. ☐
....

3 School holidays are too long. ☐
....

4 I'm as tall as my English teacher. ☐
....

5 I'm as polite as my best friend. ☐
....

6 This exercise is too difficult for me. ☐
....

Use your English

5 Circle the correct words.

Clueless and Holmes are great detectives but they often quarrel. Clueless is not as famous [1] (as) / *than* Holmes but he thinks he is a [2] *very* / *too* clever detective. Holmes thinks she is easy-going [3] *very* / *enough* but she is often as bad-tempered [4] *as* / *enough* Clueless!

The detectives and Mrs Smith often quarrel too. Mrs Smith thinks Clueless and Holmes aren't [5] *polite* / *difficult* enough and the detectives think Mrs Smith is sometimes [6] *too* / *as* bossy.

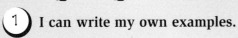

31 Friends' Club

Language Diary

1 I can write my own examples.

too much, too many, not enough	
too much	There is too much traffic in my town.
	1 There isn't too much ...
too many	There are too many people in this room.
	2 ....
not enough	She hasn't got enough money to buy a new computer.
	3 ....

2 I know these words:

crop	flood
drought	pollution
expert	climate
population	

Vocabulary

1 Complete.

Down:

1 This person knows a lot about the subject.

2 The number of people living in a place.

4 Plants we grow and eat, for example rice, fruit or vegetables.

Across:

3 This makes the environment dirty.

5 The weather a place usually has.

6 There isn't any rain at this time.

7 This happens after too much rain.

Grammar

2 Circle the correct words.

1 The farmers have got too *many* / *much* work at the moment.

2 There's always too *much* / *enough* traffic in the centre of London.

3 There aren't *much* / *enough* hotels near the sea for the tourists.

4 Too *much* / *many* rain can start a flood.

5 There aren't *much* / *enough* hospitals in this city.

6 There are too *many* / *much* cars on the roads today.

7 We haven't got *many* / *enough* water for the crops.

8 There are too *much* / *many* hotels on this island.

9 Too *much* / *many* tourism can destroy beautiful places.

10 There wasn't *many* / *enough* rain last month and now there is a drought.

3 Complete. Use *too much* or *too many*.

A Are you going to watch the film tonight?

B No, I'm not. I've got ¹too much homework.

A Please don't make ².............. noise at the party. How many people are coming?

B About thirty.

A Thirty!? That's ³.............. .

A I can't find my book.

B There are ⁴.............. things on your desk!

A There is ⁵.............. pollution in this town.

B That's because there are ⁶.............. cars on the road.

A Did you enjoy your holiday?

B No, because there were ⁷.............. tourists.

A I drank three cans of cola yesterday.

B That's ⁸..............! ⁹.............. cola isn't good for you.

A There are five cinemas in our town.

B I think that's ¹⁰.............. for a small town.

Use your English

4 Circle the correct words.

A hundred years ago a lot of people moved to the towns and ¹.............. because there wasn't ².............. work in the villages. The population in the towns grew and grew and soon there were ³.............. people in towns. Then there weren't enough houses and soon many people were hungry because there wasn't enough ⁴.............. for everybody.

These days we have a different problem. A lot of people want to live in the ⁵.............. and they drive into town every day so there is ⁶.............. traffic and the pollution is terrible.

1 A places	**B** countries	**C** cities
2 A enough	**B** not enough	**C** many
3 A too much	**B** not enough	**C** too many
4 A food	**B** meals	**C** crops
5 A outside	**B** countryside	**C** village
6 A not enough	**B** too much	**C** too many

Language Diary

 I can write my own examples.

Adverbs

He ran quickly to school.
They looked happily at their new house.
The sailors put John carefully on the deck.

1 ....
2 ....
3 ....

 I know these words:

cough (v)	land (n)
pull	rope
stare	passenger
scream	peaceful
roll	careful

Vocabulary

1 Read the definitions and find the words in the word snake.

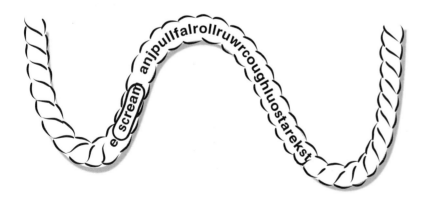

1 We sometimes do this when we're scared.
2 The opposite of push.
3 To move. To go up and down and around.
4 We usually do this when we catch a cold.
5 Look hard and for a long time at something or somebody.

2 Complete. Use the words in the box.

> land   passenger   rope
> peaceful   ~~careful~~

1 Be ...careful..! A huge wave is coming.
2 Lizzie was a .... on the *Mayflower*.
3 The Pilgrims were .... people and didn't fight with the Indians.
4 After a long voyage the Pilgrims finally saw .... It was America!
5 The sailors used a .... to pull John from the sea.

Grammar

3 Circle the correct words.

1 The ships was sailing *slow /* *slowly* to America.

2 There was a *dangerous / dangerously* storm.

3 John's head disappeared *quick / quickly* under the water.

4 Lizzie saw the new land and felt *sad / sadly*.

5 At first the Pilgrims weren't very *happy / happily* in America.

6 The Pilgrims didn't have an *easy / easily* life in America.

4 Rewrite the sentences. Use the words in CAPITALS.

1 The sailors pulled John from   SAFELY
the water. He was safe.
The sailors pulled John *safely from the water*.

2 John gave Lizzie a weak smile.   WEAKLY
John .... at Lizzie.

3 Lizzie looked at John and she felt   SADLY
sad.
Lizzie .... at John.

4 John said in a soft voice to   SOFTLY
Lizzie: 'Marry me!'
John .... to Lizzie: 'Marry me!'

5 Make adverbs from the adjectives. Then complete the text.

heavy   *heavily*
good   ....
hard   ....
peaceful   ....
quick   ....

At first the Pilgrims slept on the ship because it snowed ¹*heavily* . Then they started to build their houses. They worked very ²......... and finished them ³......... .

One day, two Indians came to see the Pilgrims. One of them could speak English ⁴......... . The Pilgrims wanted to live ⁵......... with the Indians and were friendly to them. The Indians were also friendly and they showed the Pilgrims the different crops in America.

Use your English

6 Complete. Use the correct form of the words in CAPITALS.

1 This voyage is going to be   DANGER
very *dangerous* .

2 The Pilgrims built their   CAREFUL
houses ....

3 All the .... worked   SAIL
very hard on the ship.

4 They couldn't see John   APPEAR
because he .... under
the water.

5 The *Mayflower* .... to   TURN
England without the Pilgrims
and John.

6 The Pilgrims were   FRIEND
.... to the Indians.

Check Yourself

Units 29 - 32

1 Match the opposites.

0	rude	e	**a**	difficult
1	strong	☐	**b**	dangerous
2	kind	☐	**c**	bad-tempered
3	good-tempered	☐	**d**	weak
4	safe	☐	**e**	polite
5	easy-going	☐	**f**	unkind

Total ☐ 5

2 Circle the correct words.

0 The actors wore wonderful Chinese *intervals* / *costumes* in the play.

1 The girl *played* / *screamed* because she saw a mouse.

2 The *population* / *people* of that town is about 25,000.

3 My sister sings in the school *choir* / *orchestra*.

4 It's very hot here so you can *put on* / *take off* your jacket.

5 It rained a lot and there was a *drought* / *flood*.

Total ☐ 5

Grammar

3 Complete. Use the correct question tags.

0 He's just telephoned, ...hasn't he.. ?

1 He shouldn't get up so late, ... ?

2 They didn't fall into the water, ... ?

3 She isn't crying, ... ?

4 That woman was staring at me, ... ?

5 They are going to buy a house, ... ?

6 He won't return to England, ... ?

7 They haven't eaten dinner yet, ... ?

8 The children have to put on their coats, ... ?

9 You don't want milk in your tea, ... ?

10 I'm too fat, ... ?

Total ☐ 10

4 Complete. Use *too, enough, too much* or *too many*.

0 I haven't got ..enough.. money to go to the theatre.

1 I drank .... cola and I didn't feel well.

2 My tea is .... weak and it isn't sweet .... for me.

3 There were .... people at the party and some of them sat on the floor.

Total ☐ 8

5 Tick ✓ true. Cross ✗ false.

Suzie   Jane

0 Suzie is as tall as Jane. ✗

1 Suzie's hair is as long as Jane's hair. ☐

2 Suzie isn't as thin as Jane. ☐

3 Suzie's nose isn't as small as Jane's nose. ☐

4 Suzie's bag is as big as Jane's bag. ☐

Total ☐ 8

6 Complete.

	adjective	adverb
0	careful	carefully
1	....	late
2	early	....
3	peaceful	....
4	heavy	....

Total ☐ 4

Vocabulary	10
Grammar	30
Total	40

Skills Corner 8

Reading

1 Read. Complete with headings a–f.

a A Geography lesson   d Tired but happy
b An early start   e Spend, spend, spend
c Not enough time   f Food and then home

A day out in London

1 b

Last week I went to London for the day with my friend Kate and her family. We got up at six o'clock and the train left at seven o'clock. The journey wasn't too long – three hours!

2

In the morning we went to the Science Museum. It was brilliant, but there was a problem. There were too many things to do and not enough time. We stayed there all morning so at one o'clock we were very hungry. It was a lovely day and we had a picnic in the park.

3

Kate took some photographs in the park and we also went to Oxford Street. We went shopping. I bought a T-shirt and some postcards and Kate bought some CDs.

4

We went on a boat trip down the River Thames. We saw the Thames flood barrier. It was very interesting. They built it in 1984 because sometimes there was too much rain and there were floods in London.

5

After that we went to a restaurant and I had a huge pizza and an ice cream. I ate too much but I didn't eat as much as Kate! Then we rushed to the station for our train home.

6

On the way home Kate fell asleep. I wasn't as tired as her and I listened to music. We arrived home at midnight. It was a wonderful day.

Writing

2 Read the notes. Write about Oliver and Anna's day out in your notebook.

Paragraph 1
- yesterday Oliver and Anna / go to the zoo with their class
- the bus / leave at nine o'clock
- eat sandwiches on the bus

Paragraph 2
- arrive at ten o'clock
- see lots of animals / throw fish to feed the penguins
- ride on an elephant

Paragraph 3
- get back on the bus
- the monkeys / climb on the bus and open the window
- one monkey / climb through the window / take a banana from Anna / very funny
- Oliver / take photos

Paragraph 4
- on the way home / sing songs
- stop for ice cream and drinks
- the children / sleep on the bus
- arrive home at eight o'clock

Yesterday Oliver and Anna went to the zoo with their class.

FOLLOW THE CRAZY DETECTIVES

Start Shirley Holmes and George Clueless are looking for Keith the Thief. They're running out of their house in **Baker Street**, a famous street in London. It's famous because Sherlock Holmes lived there!

Square 3 The detectives hop into a **London black cab** – a big, black taxi – to follow Keith the Thief!

Square 6 All models in **Madame Tussaud's Waxwork Museum** are made of wax, aren't they?

Square 9 Holmes can't see Keith the Thief in **Piccadilly Circus** so she decides to take a photo of Eros, the statue of the god of love.

Square 12 The detectives are next to the **Houses of Parliament** and its famous clock, **Big Ben**. 'It's three o'clock,' says Clueless. 'Time for a cup of tea.' 'Yes,' says Shirley 'but I can't hear the chimes of Big Ben!'

Square 15 Now the detectives are looking for Keith the Thief on the **River Thames**. 'Oh dear!' says Clueless. 'I think it's starting to rain!'

Square 17 Perhaps Keith the Thief is on that **London red double-decker bus** or perhaps he isn't!

Square 21 'Well, Keith the Thief isn't in **Trafalgar Square!**' says Clueless. 'Never mind! I'll take a photo of Lord Nelson's statue. He was a famous English admiral.'

Square 23 Is Keith the Thief at the new **Globe Theatre**? 'I've lost my skull!' says an actor. 'Oh, did Shakespeare write that?' says Clueless.

Square 25 'Your hat is funny,' says Clueless to the guard at the **Tower of London**.

Square 28 'But your hat is funnier!' says Holmes to the guard at **Buckingham Palace**.

Square 30 'Well done!' says the Queen of England. 'You've caught Keith the Thief!' 'Yes, here he is … Oh, where is he?' says Shirley. What clever detectives!

Game Instructions

1 Throw the dice and move your counter on the board game.

2 If you have thrown:

   1 answer a Londoners question.*
   2 answer a Crazy Detectives question.*
   3 answer a Friends' Club question.*
   4 answer a Story Time question.*
   5 sing a song or say a chant from the book.
   6 have a second turn.

*If there are no more questions, throw the dice again.

3 If you can answer your question without the clue, you get **2 points**. If you find the answer with the clue, you get **1 point**.

4 Record your points.

5 When the first player arrives at square 30, he or she gets two extra points. Then stop the game and count your points. The winner is the person with the most points.

Here are the questions!!!

The Londoners

1 What are the four countries in Great Britain? (clue: look in Unit 1)

2 How many people were there in London in 1905? (clue: look in Unit 5)

3 Which is the biggest forest in the south of England? (clue: look in Unit 9)

4 Who is Luciano Pavarotti? (clue: look in Unit 13)

5 What is RSPCA and what does it do? (clue: look in Unit 17)

6 When did the original Globe Theatre burn down? (clue: look in Unit 21)

Crazy Detectives

1 Why does Holmes enjoy looking at the furniture in her house? (clue: look in Unit 2)

2 What game did Lord Rich want to play with Clueless? (clue: look in Unit 6)

3 What five things did the burglars steal from Holmes's house? (clue: look in Unit 10)

4 What was the name of Holmes's fortune teller? (clue: look in Unit 14)

5 Has Holmes ever eaten snails? (clue: look in Unit 18)

6 What's Clueless's new hobby? (clue: look in Unit 22)

Friends' Club

1 What do pandas eat? (clue: look in Unit 3)

2 What four pieces of equipment do you need for walking? (clue: look in Unit 7)

3 Which is the largest continent? (clue: look in Unit 11)

4 What is the email address of the *Friends' Club*? (clue: look in Unit 15)

5 Which sea animal has got over one hundred teeth? (clue: look in Unit 19)

6 What does *Aibo* mean? (clue: look in Unit 27)

Story Time

1 What did the Westpark Comprehensive School football team need? (clue: look in Unit 4)

2 What did the Brown's Building Company want to build in Upton Wood? (clue: look in Unit 8)

3 Who was the ruler of Planet Kitra? (clue: look in Unit 20)

4 What machine did Dan and Joe find at the end of a tunnel outside the conversion room? (clue: look in Unit 24)

5 What was the name of the Pilgrims' ship? (clue: look in Unit 28)

6 How many Pilgrims were there at the end of their first winter in America? (clue: look in Unit 32)

Check Yourself Answers

Units 1-4

1 1 a   2 f   3 b   4 d   5 e

2 1 country   2 lake   3 swim   4 squirrel
5 football

3 1 We aren't listening to the headmaster now.
2 They don't speak English at work.
3 The Londoners don't live in Wales.
4 I'm not doing my Maths homework now.
5 A panda doesn't eat rice.
6 She isn't sleeping at the moment.

4 1 Are they cleaning   5 is making
2 is coming   6 do
3 is shouting   7 are they going
4 Does your friend play   8 do you go

5 1 Do you need   5 are cutting down
2 is ringing   6 lives
3 are you wearing   7 'm cleaning
4 doesn't snow   8 hear

Units 5-8

1 1 torch   2 map   3 compass   4 paddle
5 life jacket

2 1 traffic lights   2 zebra crossing   3 traffic
4 office block   5 double-decker bus

3 1 were   2 wasn't   3 were there   4 weren't

4 1 got on   5 decided
2 didn't rain   6 ate
3 didn't enjoy   7 drank
4 saw

5 1 Where did her friend sleep?
2 What did he read?
3 What time did they meet their friends?
4 What did the workmen measure?

6 1 go   2 knocked   3 are putting up   4 won

Units 9-12

1 1 reporter   2 march   3 mountain   4 shy
5 Equator

2 1 short   2 small   3 thin   4 pretty   5 short

3 1 prettier   the prettiest
2 more colourful   the most colourful
3 worse   the worst
4 hotter   the hottest

4 1 Ø Australia is ...   4 ... the Sun.
2 ... the Moon ...   5 ... Ø South America.
3 ... the best ...

5 1 a, The   2 Ø   3 the   4 a, Ø   5 The
6 a   7 Ø

6 1 Is Mike going to   5 are they going to
2 is   6 not going to
3 are you going to   7 Is she going to
4 'm going to   8 isn't

Units 13-16

1 <u>nouns:</u>   comet, fisherman, husband
<u>adjectives:</u> bossy, hopeless, amazing, crazy
<u>verbs:</u>   disappear, arrive, believe

2 1 space   2 queue   3 bunch   4 cold   5 emails

3 1 don't have to   4 doesn't have to
2 have to   5 don't have to
3 Do you have to

4 1 'll arrive   4 Will I marry
2 won't connect   5 will never lose
3 'll travel

5 1 of   2 about   3 with   4 at   5 in

6 1 When will Kate marry John?
2 What's his dad writing?
3 Where is the spaceship going to crash?
4 Why did he laugh?
5 How many earthquakes were there last year?

Units 17-20

1 <u>person:</u> owner, guard, vet, volunteer, ruler
<u>animal:</u> puppy, shark, crab, seal, whale

2 1 e   2 a   3 c   4 f   5 b

3 1 Has Kate cleaned   4 fed
2 cleaned   5 haven't brushed
3 did you feed   6 brushed

4 1 eaten   2 caught   3 won   4 known
5 been

5 1 never   2 yet   3 just   4 yet   5 never
6 just   7 yet   8 ever

6 1 any-   2 any-   3 No-   4 no-   5 any-

Units 21–24

1 1 eating   2 horse   3 machine
4 bored with   5 organise

2 1 collection   2 escape   3 quarrel
4 explain   5 programme

3 1 Can / Could   4 Can / Could
2 Can / Could   5 Would you like
3 Would you like   6 Can / Could

4 1 Let's   2 Why don't   3 What about
4 Let's not

5 1 What is your friend good at?
2 What is he very fond of?
3 Is your dad keen on canoeing?
4 What is she crazy about?

6 1 shouldn't   2 shouldn't   3 should
4 should

Units 25–28

1 1 b   2 e   3 c   4 a

2 1 cuts   2 water   3 planted   4 dug
5 grow   6 Gardening

3 1 Were you playing
2 were you doing
3 wasn't cleaning
4 Were your parents working
5 wasn't sleeping, was listening
6 Was she doing
7 Was she watching

4 1 was cleaning, was sleeping
2 was buying, left
3 was sailing, fell
4 was doing, heard

5 1 couldn't   2 couldn't, can
3 Will people be able

6 1 saw   6 was looking at
2 was   7 was playing
3 had   8 shouted
4 could   9 was
5 couldn't   10 was walking

Units 29–32

1 1 d   2 f   3 c   4 b   5 a

2 1 screamed   2 population   3 choir
4 take off   5 flood

3 1 should he   6 will he
2 did they   7 have they
3 is she   8 don't they
4 wasn't she   9 do you
5 aren't they   10 aren't I

4 1 too much   2 too, enough   3 too many

5 1 ✗   2 ✓   3 ✓   4 ✗
1 late   2 early   3 peacefully   4 heavily

Game Answers

The Londoners

1 England, Scotland, Wales and Northern Ireland.
2 More than six million.
3 The New Forest.
4 A famous Italian singer.
5 The Royal Society for the Prevention of Cruelty to Animals. This organisation finds new homes for about 80, 000 stray animals every year.
6 Over 400 years ago.

Crazy Detectives

1 Because she likes looking for fingerprints.
2 Chess.
3 Furniture, paintings, books, jewellery and clothes.
4 Madame Rosa.
5 No, she hasn't.
6 Collecting stamps.

Friends' Club

1 Bamboo.
2 A compass, a map, walking boots and a rucksack.
3 Asia.
4 www.longman.com/friends
5 A dolphin.
6 *Pal* or *partner*.

Story Time

1 A new football pitch.
2 Shops, office blocks, new roads and a roundabout.
3 Azdie.
4 A transporter.
5 The *Mayflower*.
6 Fifty-two.

Pearson Education Limited,
Edinburgh Gate, Harlow,
Essex, CM20 2JE, England
and Associated Companies throughout the world.

www.pearsonelt.com/friends

First published 2003
Twentieth impression 2018
Set in Slimbach 11pt

Printed in Italy by L.E.G.OOS.p.A.

ISBN: 978-0-582-30659-2

Illustrated by: Gary Andrews, Jo Blake (Beehive Illustration), Andrew Clark,
Mark Davis (Mackerel Creative Services), Kes Hankin (Gemini Design),
Peter Richardson, Stephanie Strickland, Mark Vallance (Gemini Design),
Ross Watton

Design and page make-up by Gemini Design

We are grateful to the following for permission to reproduce the photographs:
A1pix pages 41, 51 (rhino); Trevor Clifford pages 13, 23, 42, 73; Bruce Coleman
Collection page 46 (dolphin); Corbis/Rob Lewine page 61; Corbis/Chris Collins
page 67 bottom right; DK Images pages 46 (seal), 46 (shark); Deutsches
Museum page 67 top right; Leslie Garland Picture Library page 27; ImageState
pages 46 (octopus), 51 (hippo), 67 bottom left; Impact/Mark Henley page 77;
Peter Lake pages 17 right, 37; Pictures Colour Library page 46 (crab); Science
Photo Library/Volker Steger page 67 top left; The Stockmarket page 81;
Stone/Keren Stu page 7; Stone/Nicholas Parfitt page 51 (elephant); SuperStock
page 31; Taxi/Arthur Tilley page 43; Topham Picturepoint page 17 left; Stuart
Westmorland page 46 (whale).

All photographs not listed above are ©Pearson Education/Peter Lake.

Cover photograph ©Pearson Education/by Peter Lake.